Collins *rambler's guide*

isle of skye

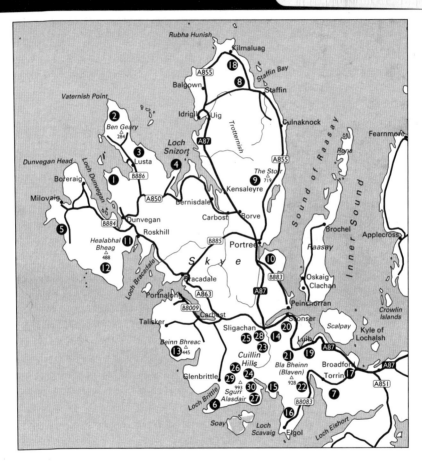

The Ramblers' Association, because it does not have a presence on the Isle of Skye, has not been able to check the text or maps in this book. Therefore, unlike most other titles in this series, the Association can take no responsibility for the accuracy of the walks provided. It endorses the series as a whole and fully expects this volume to be of an equally high standard to that of the other titles in the series.

The Ramblers

ARVEY

chris townsend

HarperCollins*Publishers*
77–85 Fulham Palace Road
London W6 8JB

The HarperCollins website address is:

www.**fire**and**water**.com

06 05 04 03 02 01

8 7 6 5 4 3 2 1

First published 2001

Series Editor Richard Sale

ISBN 0 00 220200 X

Designed and produced by Drum Enterprises Ltd.
Printed and bound in Great Britain by Scotprint

CONTENTS

INTRODUCTION

Skye is a beautiful island of cliff-rimmed promontories, remote beaches, long sea lochs, jagged rock peaks, steep stony hills, long high ridges and rolling moorland. Most especially, it contains the most rugged, rocky and magnificent mountain range in Britain, the superlative Cuillin. There are also more gentle hills scattered over the island and in the north the long Trotternish ridge with a series of amazing landslips on its eastern flanks. The coast has spectacular cliff scenery, arguably the most impressive in Britain, with sea stacks, caves, arches, waterfalls and other features.

GEOLOGY AND GEOGRAPHY

Skye is the second largest and best known of the Hebrides, some 640 sq. miles (1,600km^2) in area and measuring roughly 50 miles (80km) by 25 miles (40km). Over a dozen large sea lochs bite into the island, giving it a hugely indented shape that means that nowhere on Skye is more than 5 miles (8km) from the sea and the coastline is over 350 miles (570km) long.

Long peninsulas stretch out between the sea lochs – Sleat, Minginish, Duirinish, Waternish and Trotternish. These give Skye one of its names – An t-Eilean Sgiathanach, the Winged Isle, a huge eagle swooping down to seize its prey. It's also know as Eilean a'Cheo, the Misty Isle, after the low clouds that often drift across it. To the people of Skye it's simply An t-Eilean, The Island. The meaning of Skye itself is now unknown. It may come from the Gaelic 'sgiath' meaning 'wing' or perhaps the Norse 'skuy' meaning 'mist'.

Skye lies close to the western seaboard of the Scottish mainland to which it is now linked at Kyleakin by a controversial toll bridge. You can still travel to Skye by ferry though, from Mallaig to Armadale or Glenelg to Kylerhea. The bridge is the convenient if expensive way to reach the island but it's the ferries that give a feel of adventure and magic to the journey.

Geologically Skye is fascinating and complex and a favourite place for geology students to come and study. The oldest rocks on Skye are sedimentary rocks, mainly found on the Sleat peninsula. The larger part of the island is made up of volcanic rocks however with a vast sheet of lava, mostly basalt, covering most of the north and west of the island. Erosion of this lava plateau resulted in flat-topped hills such as Macleod's Tables. In Trotternish the basalt sheet is tilted with the raised scarp slope to the east, pressing down on the rocks below. The pinnacles, towers and other fantastic features found along the eastern edge of the Trotternish ridge are due to landslides caused by weaker sedimentary rocks collapsed under the weight of this thick layer of basalt. In some areas large volcanoes appeared. Erosion has removed most of these volcanoes leaving behind just the roots in the form of the Red Hills and the Cuillin, the first being mostly gabbro, the latter granite.

Erosion in fact has been the main force in shaping the landscape as it is today. In particular erosion by ice during the ice ages when ice sheets and glaciers covered most of Skye. The Cuillin in particular show the effects of glaciation with ice-carved smooth slabs, hanging valleys, truncated spurs, knife-edge ridges and other features.

HISTORY

Skye has a long, complex and interesting history and it's only possible to touch on a few main strands here. The classic reference book is Alexander Nicolson's History of Skye.

The Coire Lagan skyline from the path above Loch Brittle

Descending to the shores of
Loch Eishort between Suisnish
and Boreraig

The first people started to settle in the Hebrides some 1,500 years after the last ice age ended 10,000 years ago. There are few remnants of these first Stone Age hunter-gatherer people on Skye but the farmers that followed them left more relics in the form of chambered cairns, standing stones and stone circles.

For thousands of years the peoples of Skye do not appear to have built fortifications. However some 3,000 years ago the first hillforts appeared, presumably due to an increase in conflict. Large hillforts were the norm for many centuries but then they began to be replaced by smaller constructions, often just a wall across a headland, that are known as duns. Then just over 2,000 years ago the impressive Iron Age circular fortifications, called brochs, started to appear. There are several good examples of these on Skye (see Walk 2). Early in the 1st century AD these were abandoned, suggesting a more peaceable period, probably due to the Roman occupation of southern Britain drawing away the attentions of potential invaders.

The Celtic people living on Skye at the time of the brochs and through the first 500 years AD were known as Picts, a term first used by the Romans for all the people of the Highlands and Islands. The Scots arrived from Ireland in the years following 500 AD, with Christianity arriving soon afterwards, St Columba reaching Skye in 585 AD. A few centuries after this the Viking invasions began, resulting in Skye being ruled by them for over four centuries. There are few physical signs of the Vikings. They left their mark in the form of many place and hill names.

Norse rule ended in 1263 when King Hakon of Norway was defeated by the Scots at the battle of Largs. In 1266 Skye and the rest of the Hebrides became part of Scotland. However under the leadership of the Lord of the Isles there was much resistance to Scottish rule for the next few centuries. There was also much inter-clan warfare, especially between the Macleods and the MacDonalds, which lasted until 1601 when a final battle was fought in Coire na Creich in the Cuillin. After this James V1 called the clan chiefs together and forced them to accept arbitration.

Neither the Macleods or the MacDonalds, the leading clans on Skye, supported the Jacobites in the uprising of 1745 so Skye wasn't devastated afterwards in the way other areas were. Bonnie Prince Charlie did pass through Skye while on the run from government forces after his army was defeated at the battle of Culloden (1746). In a famous incident he was rowed to Skye from South Uist by Flora MacDonald.

In the aftermath of the Jacobite uprising the clan chiefs lost their powers to raise armies. The value of the clan lands lay now solely in the money they could bring in not in the people who lived there. This income was initially in the form of rent.

Due to a number of factors including the introduction of the potato and vaccination against smallpox the population of Skye increased after the '45 reaching a peak in the 1830s and 40s.

The Quiraing and Meall na
Suirnach from the south

The potato quickly became the staple item of food, which meant that poor potato harvests in the mid-1830s led to many people becoming destitute. Further harvest failures in the 1846 and subsequent years made the situation much worse. For the landlords it meant much reduced income, as many people were unable to pay their rent. Sheep however could bring in money but to graze sheep required combining the small crofts into larger areas. Sheep didn't require many people to look after them either so there was no work for most of the crofters in sheep farming. The result was the enforced evictions known as the Clearances as the landlords replaced the people with sheep. People were driven from their homes, which were often burnt down so they could not return. With nowhere else to go thousands of people were forced to emigrate, many dying of disease or in shipwrecks. Evidence of this notorious and shameful period of history can be found in many places on Skye. Walk 7 visits two villages, Suisnish and Boreraig, that were destroyed in the Clearances. For those interested in this subject David Craig's superb On the Crofter's Trail is recommended reading.

The Clearances lasted from the 1840s to the 1870s. In the 1880s remaining crofters began to protest at their treatment by the landowners and there were several major confrontations between crofters and the police that received massive publicity. This led to the Napier Commission and the Crofting Act of 1886, which gave many rights to crofters. Much more recent legislation has given crofters the right to purchase their land and there is now a movement for local communities to have control over crofting land.

At the same time as the crofters were fighting for their rights the first mountaineers were arriving. General tourism can be said to have begun a hundred years earlier with the journeys of Thomas Pennant and then Samuel Johnson and James Boswell. Sir Walter Scott's visit to Coruisk in 1814 further encouraged the growth of tourism. Today walking, climbing and other forms of tourism are very important to the economy of Skye.

NATURAL HISTORY
Skye is a superb place for bird watchers and botanists with an interesting and varied fauna and flora. One reason for this is the undeveloped nature of most of the island, another the many different habitats of coasts, woodland, grassland, moorland and high mountains.

FLORA
Little is left of the woodland that once covered much of the island. The change to a cooler, wetter climate some 5,000 years ago, clearance for fields and dwellings and grazing by sheep and cattle all played their part in the removal of the forest. Regeneration is being encouraged in a few places (see Walk 7) and there are still some native woods of birch, hazel, alder, rowan, ash and oak remaining. Most of the forests though are commercial ones, rigid blocks of conifers that stand out as unnatural intrusions in the landscape. Native woodlands are often carpeted with moss and lichen. Where the trees grow on well-drained limestone primroses, bluebells, wood anemones and meadowsweet can be found.

The woods were replaced by the vast moorlands of blanket peat bog that cover much of the island away from the coast. Various grasses and heathers dominate the moors. Cotton grass with its fully white flowerheads grows in the wettest areas as does yellow bog asphodel. The low yellow flowers of tormentil are common on slightly drier ground. Bog myrtle, a small shrub, is abundant too and there are large areas of sphagnum moss. Other plants you are likely to find include devilsbit scabious, bogbean, sundew, common butterwort and heath spotted orchid.

View down a gully on the Storr to the Storr Sanctuary and Loch Leathan

The moors run right up to the coasts but there are often dry grassy strips with grassland flowers here while on the cliffs and rocky beaches plants such as the fleshy roseroot, sea campion and thrift can be found.

In limestone areas, such as around Loch Slapin, the ground is well drained and there is grassland rather than bogland. This grassland is rich in flowers, including thyme, bird's foot trefoil, selfheal and more.

Above the moors on the rocky slopes of the mountains where soil is thin you can find blaeberry, least willow, mountain everlasting, heath bedstraw, crowberry and juniper. In the gullies and on the ledges saxifrages, moss campion and other alpine flowers grow.

FAUNA

The richest bird and animal life is to be found round the coasts. On the beaches waders such as curlew and oystercatcher are common along with various species of gulls and terns. Herons are often seen in estuaries and bays too. Fulmars and kittiwakes nest on the cliffs, sometimes in great numbers, as do guillemots and razorbills on the sea stacks and small islands just off the coast. Cormorants and shags, large dark fish-eating birds, can be seen flying low over the sea or perched on small rocks and islets holding their wings out to dry. Walkers with binoculars can see many more species out on the sea.

Seals are numerous and often seen, either bobbing in the water watching you curiously or lying on rocky islets. Dolphins and porpoises can be seen cruising offshore too. Otters also live on the coast but are difficult to see.

Many woodland animals have had to adapt to more open country and are now found on moorland and even high in the mountains. Red deer are perhaps the best known example. There are fewer of these on Skye than in many mainland areas but they can be seen in places, including some of the quieter Cuillin corries. The other deer found on Skye is the roe deer but this is only found in woodland. Rabbits live in the woods but also out in the open. Many grassy cliff edges are riddled with rabbit burrows. Foxes roam the whole island from coast to mountain but being mainly nocturnal are not that often seen. Other predators are stoats and weasels.

Moorland and grassland birds include curlew, snipe, golden plover, meadow pipit, skylark, merlin, kestrel, hen harrier and short-eared owl. Peregrine falcons, buzzards, ravens and golden eagles hunt and scavenge on the moors too but can also be found on the coasts and high in the mountains. Indeed, ravens are likely to be seen on every walk in this book. Their smaller relative the hooded crow or hoodie is frequently seen too. Buzzards are very common. However the magnificent golden eagle, whilst not rare, is less frequently seen. Red grouse are less common than on the mainland though they can startle you at times with their harsh cries as they explode out of the heather almost at your feet. Their smaller, quieter relative, the ptarmigan, is mostly found on the Red Hills.

The beautiful red-throated diver nests on some moorland lochs. These birds are easily disturbed and should only be watched from a distance. On the larger inland lochs whooper swans arrive in the winter from the arctic.

There are many more birds to be seen and it is well worth the walker interested in wildlife carrying a lightweight pair of binoculars. There are many models that weigh no more than 5–8oz (150–225g) and which can be easily carried in a jacket pocket.

ACCESS
Access to wild country is not a problem on Skye and there are no restrictions at any time of the year on any of the walks described. Walkers should take care to close gates and not damage walls or fences or disturb livestock of course.

THE WALKER AND THE ENVIRONMENT
PATH EROSION
Walking in the countryside is an increasingly popular pastime. In general the impact of walkers on the landscape is small. However path erosion is a growing problem, especially on the often boggy and therefore easily eroded approaches to hills. Path repairs have been carried out in many areas and are needed in many others. This is an expensive and sometimes intrusive remedy however. Whilst sheer numbers alone can cause erosion, much damage to paths is the result of bad walking practices.

MINIMISING PATH EROSION
The main way to reduce damage to paths is to stay on them, preferably in the centre. Walking on the edges breaks these down and widens the path, leading to a spreading, unsightly scar. Even when paths are wet and muddy you should stay on them. If you're concerned about wet feet, wear gaiters and proof your boots well. Even then, keeping your feet dry may be impossible in wet conditions. Outside of winter conditions, I wear lightweight footwear that dries quickly and just accept that my feet will get wet.

A common cause of erosion on steep hillsides is where people have cut the corners of zigzags, creating a channel down which water can run. Although it's very tempting to do this, especially in descent, it's important to stay on the path.

WALKING OFF PATHS
Where there are no paths care should be taken to leave as

Lorgasdal Bay

little trace of your passing as possible. Rocks, gravel and other hard surfaces are more resistant to wear than soft, wet ground. Dry grass or heather covered slopes stand up to impact better than boggy areas.

CAIRNS

Marking cross country routes with cairns detracts from the feeling of being in wild country and can also lead to paths appearing where there were none before as other walkers follow them. There are far too many cairns on established paths too, so many indeed that they can cause confusion rather than help with route finding. I often knock down cairns and never build them. Summit cairns and cairns on prominent points, many of which are very old and have cultural and historical associations, are another matter and should be left alone. Cairns covered with lichen or moss are a sign of antiquity as are ones that have been carefully constructed rather than just piled up. With new cairns the holes the stones were prised from may still be visible. If so the stones should be replaced as far as possible.

CAMPING

Camping in wild country far from civilisation is a wonderful experience. It can cause damage if done carelessly however. The aim of all wild campers should be to leave no trace of their presence. With modern lightweight equipment this isn't difficult.

Two practices that aren't necessary if you know how to choose a good site and how to pitch your tent properly are using rocks to hold down tent pegs and digging drainage trenches round a tent. I camp in the hills regularly and never do either of these. Rocks on pegs is by far the commoner of the two practices and I have all too often spent time dismantling the unsightly rings of stones left by other campers. If you do ever put rocks on tent pegs or decide to move those left by others either replace the rocks in their original holes if these can be seen or else spread them out over a rocky or vegetation free area or even dump them in the nearest stream.

Campers should always use stoves. Campfires damage the ground and leave long-lasting scars as well as being inefficient.

TOILETS

There is nothing more sordid than seeing pink and white strands of used toilet paper sticking out from a pile of faeces lying in the grass or half-hidden under a rock. As well as being unpleasant to see, the unthinking disposal of human waste can pollute water supplies and cause illness. Ideally, toilets should be sited at least 200 yards from the nearest water. Where this isn't possible due to the prevalence of tiny streams and boggy pools head uphill and away from the main watercourses. You should keep well away from any paths or obvious walking routes such as ridge crests too. Unless there is a risk of fire toilet paper should be burnt. A lighter or box of matches can be carried in the plastic bag with the paper for this purpose. Faeces should be covered by stones or loose vegetation or, even better, buried. Small plastic or metal lightweight trowels are available for this. When carried, an ice axe makes a good trenching tool. In soft soil the heel of a boot can be used. The hole doesn't need to be deep. Indeed, decomposition takes place more quickly near the surface so 4–6in (10–15cm) is fine.

LITTER

All rubbish should be packed out. This includes orange peel and other biodegradable material as this can attract scavenging birds such as crows and gulls into the hills where they may then devastate local bird populations by eating the young and eggs. Removing other peoples litter is good practice. Carrying a small plastic bag for this is worthwhile. Burning rubbish is not acceptable. Aside from the likelihood that it won't all be consumed the fire itself will leave a scar and could get out of control.

MOUNTAIN BIKES

Mountain bikes can be useful for long approaches to the hills. Their use on vehicle tracks is fine but on paths and off-road they can cause great erosion, especially when the ground is wet.

DOGS

Dogs taken on the hills must be kept under control and not allowed to chase animals, whether wild or domestic. During lambing season, from March to May, they should be left at home as even the presence of a well-behaved dog can upset pregnant sheep.

WEATHER

Skye has a reputation for rain and mist though in fact it has on average more sunshine than many areas on the mainland with 1,200 hours per year. The weather varies from place to place to with the north of the island being drier than the south and the east warmer than the west. Average rainfall on the coast is 47in (120cm) while high in the mountains it's over twice that at 118in (300cm). The Cuillin is often cloudy or wet when much of the rest of the island is dry.

The climate is cool but not cold, with an average summer temperature of 59°F (16°C). Winters are mild and wet. Low level snow is very rare but significant amounts can build up high in the mountains.

On average spring has the driest weather with summer being wetter but this doesn't hold true every year. Indeed, Skye's weather changes rapidly so making predictions even for the next day is very difficult. Because of the variation in conditions in different parts of the islands flexible plans will allow the walker to make the best of the weather.

SAFETY

Much of Skye consists of rough, difficult terrain where progress can be slow. It can be a long way, in time if not in distance, from the nearest road or habitation.

This is not to say that walking on Skye is a risky pastime. Even on the Cuillin only a tiny minority of walkers ever gets into difficulties. Sensible preparation is needed however for all the walks described in this book. Being able to navigate accurately with map and compass is essential. Note though that the compass can be unreliable in the Cuillin, as some of the rocks are magnetic. This problem can be minimised by holding the compass high up and away from rocks and taking several readings from different points.

Looking down to Sgurr nan Gillean from Druim nan Ramh

Adequate footwear is very important as most accidents in the wilds are caused by simple slips. Wellingtons may be fine for short walks on low level footpaths but once you venture higher and further then proper walking boots or shoes are needed. A small rucksack should always be carried, containing at the minimum a waterproof jacket and trousers (if not worn), spare sweater, hat and gloves, food and drink, small first aid kit, safety whistle, map and compass. For longer walks a plastic survival bag and a torch (with spare batteries) are also recommended. An ice axe and crampons, and the skill to use them, are required in winter conditions for hill walks. The short daylight hours of winter need taking into account too.

MOUNTAIN RESCUE

The Skye Mountain Rescue team is a voluntary body and relies on donations for funding. Collecting boxes can be found in outdoor shops, cafes, bars and other places throughout the area. Please contribute if you can.

If an accident occurs priority must be given to ensuring the safety of those not involved before giving first aid to the injured. This means ensuring that people keep warm and dry and aren't somewhere exposed to danger from avalanches or rockfall or perched precariously above steep drops. To call for help use the standard distress call of six blasts of a whistle or flashes of a torch repeated at intervals of a minute. If possible someone should go for help.

If you have a mobile phone this should of course be used if it will work. However there is no coverage in many areas and even where there is phones may not work in gullies, below cliffs or in other sheltered areas. This means you may have to climb high up a hillside to get a signal, which may not be advisable or even feasible in poor weather. Mobile phones should only be used if there is genuine need. If you can get yourself and your party safely off the hill this should be done. A phone is not a substitute for having the necessary skills and equipment.

To call out a rescue team dial 999 and ask for the police. You should have the following information to give them: the exact location of the incident with six figure grid reference and a description of any obvious features, the time the incident occurred, the number of casualties, a brief outline of what happened, the nature and severity of the injuries and any treatment given. This should be written down to avoid

LYME DISEASE

The Rambler's Association Factsheet 15 provides information on the above which is caused by tick bites. Although treatable, Lyme Disease can be serious if the symptoms are not properly diagnosed. For more details contact The Ramblers for a copy of the factsheet or visit their website at: www.ramblers.org.uk

mistakes. A pencil stub and some notepaper can be kept in the first aid kit for this.

Someone should stay with the injured person if possible. If they have to be left alone then the location should be marked with something bright or reflective that can quickly be spotted.

MIDGES, TICKS AND CLEGS

Midges (*Culicoides impunctatus*) are tiny biting insects that can make life miserable, unbearable even, on warm, humid days when they attack in swarms. They are a particular problem for campers. Luckily, midges can't fly in more than a light breeze and don't like heavy rain or hot sun. Calm cloudy days, especially at dawn and dusk, bring them out in their millions however. Insect repellents will stop them biting, though they still crawl maddeningly over your skin. Repellents containing a powerful chemical called DEET work well but there are health concerns to do with the use of DEET. Personally, I'd rather avoid putting anything on my skin that melts plastic watchstraps! Of the alternatives to DEET I've found Myrica, made from bog myrtle extract, and Mosi-Guard Natural, made from eucalyptus, both work well. Citronella products are not so good. Long sleeved, tightly woven clothing is also useful in protecting against midges while headnets may be essential for the sanity of campers.

Ticks are very small insects that live in long grass and bracken and can attach themselves to you or your clothing when you brush past. They then insert their mouthparts into your flesh and suck up blood, swelling as they fill. They're not the immediate irritation midges are but the bites can transmit disease. As ticks don't bite immediately a body search at the end of the day can often locate and remove them before they've broken the skin. When a tick is embedded in the flesh it needs to be removed very carefully so the mouthpiece doesn't break off and remain in the wound. A pair of tweezers is useful for this. Dabbing them with alcohol, petrol or insect repellent can encourage them to withdraw. When walking through long vegetation tucking trousers into socks and perhaps dabbing the ankles with insect repellent is a good way to prevent ticks attaching themselves. Ticks are a particular problem in early summer.

How to use this book

This book contains route maps and descriptions for 30 walks. Each walk is graded (see p.3) and areas of interest are indicated by symbols (see below). For each walk particular points of interest are denoted by a capital letter both in the text and on the map (where the letter appears in a red box). In the text the route descriptions are prefixed by lower-case letters. We recommend that you read the whole description, including the tinted box at the start of each walk, before setting out.

Key to maps

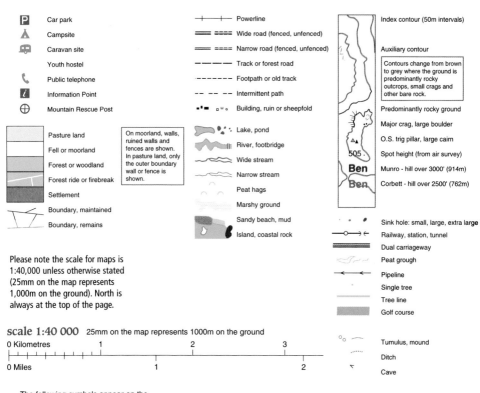

P	Car park
Å	Campsite
	Caravan site
	Youth hostel
☎	Public telephone
i	Information Point
⊕	Mountain Rescue Post

	Pasture land
	Fell or moorland
	Forest or woodland
	Forest ride or firebreak
	Settlement
	Boundary, maintained
	Boundary, remains

On moorland, walls, ruined walls and fences are shown. In pasture land, only the outer boundary wall or fence is shown.

+———+	Powerline
	Wide road (fenced, unfenced)
	Narrow road (fenced, unfenced)
— — —	Track or forest road
- - - - -	Footpath or old track
-- -- --	Intermittent path
▪■ ▫∪▫	Building, ruin or sheepfold
	Lake, pond
	River, footbridge
	Wide stream
	Narrow stream
	Peat hags
	Marshy ground
	Sandy beach, mud
	Island, coastal rock

	Index contour (50m intervals)
	Auxiliary contour

Contours change from brown to grey where the ground is predominantly rocky outcrops, small crags and other bare rock.

	Predominantly rocky ground
	Major crag, large boulder
	O.S. trig pillar, large cairn
505 ·	Spot height (from air survey)
Ben	Munro - hill over 3000' (914m)
Ben	Corbett - hill over 2500' (762m)
· · ●	Sink hole: small, large, extra large
—○—➤←	Railway, station, tunnel
	Dual carriageway
	Peat grough
←——←—	Pipeline
·	Single tree
	Tree line
	Golf course
° ° —	Tumulus, mound
········	Ditch
↰	Cave

Please note the scale for maps is 1:40,000 unless otherwise stated (25mm on the map represents 1,000m on the ground). North is always at the top of the page.

scale 1:40 000   25mm on the map represents 1000m on the ground

0 Kilometres	1	2	3

0 Miles	1	2

The following symbols appear on the maps and relate directly to the text for each walk

A Indicates a point of interest denoted by a capital letter in the text

a Indicates route instruction denoted by a lower-case letter in the text

 Geology

 Birdlife

 Other wildlife

 Wild flowers

 Literature

 Good views

 Historical interest

 Woodland

Key to symbols

At the start of each walk there is a series of symbols that indicate particular areas of interest associated with the route.

THE CORAL BEACHES AND LOVAIG BAY

START/FINISH:
Claigan car park at the end of the single track road leading north-north-west from Dunvegan. There is no public transport to Claigan or Dunvegan.

DISTANCE:
5 miles (8km)

APPROXIMATE TIME:
2–4 hours

HIGHEST POINT:
100ft (30m)

MAP:
OS Landranger 23 North Skye

REFRESHMENTS:
Dunvegan has cafes, bars and shops.

ADVICE:
An easy seaside stroll.

A short coastal walk with excellent views leads to the bright white sands of the Coral Beaches after which a brief ascent leads round a headland to the expanse of Lovaig Bay. This is a there and back again walk with plenty of opportunities to relax and enjoy the scenery. The Coral Beaches are quite popular but few people go on to Lovaig Bay.

A   Claigan 232 537
Claigan is a remote group of crofts at the end of a scenic minor road that gives wonderful views over Loch Dunvegan to MacLeod's Tables (see Walk 11). The name means 'place of cultivation'.

a   From the car park in Claigan the walk goes through a gate and down a track towards the shore where it becomes a path. This runs north, crossing rabbit and sheep cropped turf dotted with the tiny white flowers of eyebright, to the Coral Beaches.

B The Coral Beaches 225 544
The white sands of the Beaches aren't in fact made of the coral found in the tropics but from a seaweed called Lithothamnion that grows in sheltered spots around the coast. The sands are made up of tiny broken pieces of this

Approaching the Coral Beaches from Claigan

plant, washed up by the tide. In bright sunshine the sands are a startlingly white. Combined with the dark blue of the sea this can create the illusion of the shore of a tropical island rather than a North Atlantic coastline.

The coral was valuable as a lime fertiliser and used to be carried inland in large quantities to be put on acidic crofting land.

The Coral Beaches

C Cnoc Mor a'Ghrobain 225 543
A small steep sided hill with a rocky top called Cnoc Mor a'Ghrobain rises above the beach. This is worth climbing as it's a fine viewpoint for the nearby coast and south up Loch Dunvegan to the flat top of Healabhal Mhor, the northernmost of MacLeod's Tables.

b Continue round the coast from Cnoc Mor a'Ghrobain past Lampay, a small island just offshore, to the headland of Groban na Sgeire.

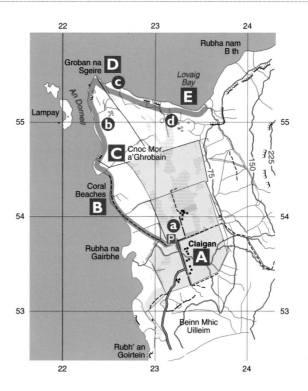

D Groban na Sgeire 223 555
The rocky headland fades into the sea in a series of long ribs of lava. When the tide is low you can venture out onto these. Just to the north lie the small islands of Isay and Mingay.

c At Groban na Sgeire a wall runs down to the sea. Round the end of this, climb a short fence and follow sheep paths just above the increasingly rugged coastline to Lovaig Bay.

E Lovaig Bay 233 552
Lovaig Bay is far less visited than the Coral Beaches and has a wilder feel. On the eastern side rise the cliffs of Rubha nam Both.

d Return to Claigan by the same route.

Looking over the Coral Beaches and Loch Dunvegan to Healabhal Mhor (Macleod's Table North)

WATERNISH POINT

START/FINISH:
Car park opposite Trumpan Church, which lies at the end of a long single track road from Stein, which is at the end of the B886 that runs north from the A850, some 6 miles (10km) north-east of Dunvegan. There is no public transport to the start of the walk.

DISTANCE:
8 miles (13km)

APPROXIMATE TIME:
3–6 hours

HIGHEST POINT:
360ft (110m)

MAP:
OS Landranger 23 North Skye

REFRESHMENTS:
Dunvegan has the nearest facilities.

ADVICE:
This walk can be very wet underfoot after rain. The walking itself is easy. As both lie in this remote part of Skye this walk could be done on the same day as Walk 3, Beinn an Sguirr.

Waternish Point lies at the end of the remote, lonely Waternish Peninsula. There are no high mountains or huge cliffs on Waternish just a wide-open landscape of moorland and ocean with vast horizons. En route to Waternish Point, where there is an automatic lighthouse, the walk passes two historical monuments, two brochs and the ruins of Unish. East of the point the coast rises to the cliffs of Creag an Fhithich from where a way can be made across low moorland back to Unish and the track to Trumpan. As well as the historical interest and the coastal scenery there are wild flowers and sea birds to be seen plus seals off the coast.

A   Trumpan Church 225 612

Trumpan is a Norse word meaning 'one sided hillock'. The story behind the ruined church is that in 1578 (or 1580 depending on the source), while the MacLeods were worshipping inside, their great enemies, the MacDonalds from the Isle of Eigg, burnt it down, which as it was thatched was easy to do. All the MacLeods, except for one woman, were killed in the fire or by the MacDonalds when they attempted to escape. The woman escaped and more MacLeods came from Dunvegan, where they had seen the smoke from the fire, and killed most of the MacDonalds who couldn't escape as their ships were stranded by the ebbing tide. The dead of both clans were buried under a stone wall or dyke, which was toppled over them, hence the affair is known as the Battle of the Spoiling of the Dyke. There are different

Looking across flower meadows to Rubha Dubh from Trumpan

versions of this story, and how historically accurate it is, is open to question.

Waternish Point

From the car park opposite the church there is a view across rich flower meadows to the cliffs, above which runs the track to Waternish Point.

a   Start the walk by turning left along the narrow road and following it to where it turns right. Turn left here through a gate onto a rough four-wheel drive vehicle track. After a few hundred yards another gate leads out onto open heather moorland where wheatears and stonechats can be seen in summer. The track heads northwards with extensive views west to the rippling low line of the Outer Hebrides. Looking back the cliffs of Dunvegan Head can be seen over Trumpan Church.

B   Memorial Cairns 233 623 and 230 632
Two tall cairns are passed as the track cuts across the moorland. Both are memorials to another battle in the bloody history of clan feuds. The first, a few hundred yards above the track on the right, is for John MacLeod of Waternish, who

WATERNISH

Waternish means a water promontory, that is one that projects into the sea, an apt name for this long, narrow and fairly low peninsula. The word is Norse, from 'vatne-nes' and hence pronounced Vaternish. 'Nish' in fact is the same word as 'ness' and comes from the Norse 'nes'.

died in a battle with the MacDonalds around 1530. The second cairn, just a few yards from the track, commemorates John MacLeod's son, Roderick, who died in the same battle. In 1985 the American branch of the Clan MacLeod rebuilt both cairns.

C Dun Borrafiach and Dun Gearymore 236 637 and 237 649

Beyond the monument cairns two brochs lie near the track. These Iron Age circular forts, built roughly around 200 BC, are associated with the Picts, the pre-Scottish inhabitants of Scotland, though not much is known about them. Broch is another Viking word, coming from 'brog', a fort. 'Dun' is a Gaelic word that means a fortified homestead. It has a much wider meaning than broch. Brochs are believed to have developed from more basic duns and are impressive examples of dry stone architecture. They are 45–65ft (13–20m) in diameter and have hollow walls. Some 11½–14½ft (3.5–4.5m) thick these walls contained staircases that led to different floors in the walls along with rooms.

Both brochs are situated above the track in defensive positions that would have been good viewpoints for the surrounding area and can be clearly seen from a distance. It's worth making the boggy diversion to the first and best preserved broch, Dun Borrafiach, which has a fine curving wall remaining on one side that shows the skill involved in its building. Dun Gearymore is closer to the track but more ruinous.

b Beyond Dun Gearymore the track starts to curve north-east towards the stark ruined house of Unish. To reach Unish leave the track at a gate on the left, go through a sheepfold then diagonally across a meadow to another gate. From the ruin you can walk across boggy moorland down to the automatic lighthouse and Waternish Point.

Alternatively, leave the track where it starts to bend north-east and follow the coastline to the lighthouse.

D Waternish Point 233 671

The stubby white lighthouse is perched on a low cliff with views out over the vast expanse of the sea. It's a good spot for watching sea birds, with cormorants and shags to be seen on the rocks below.

Bonnie Prince Charlie landed briefly near Waternish Point after his crossing from South Uist with Flora MacDonald. An

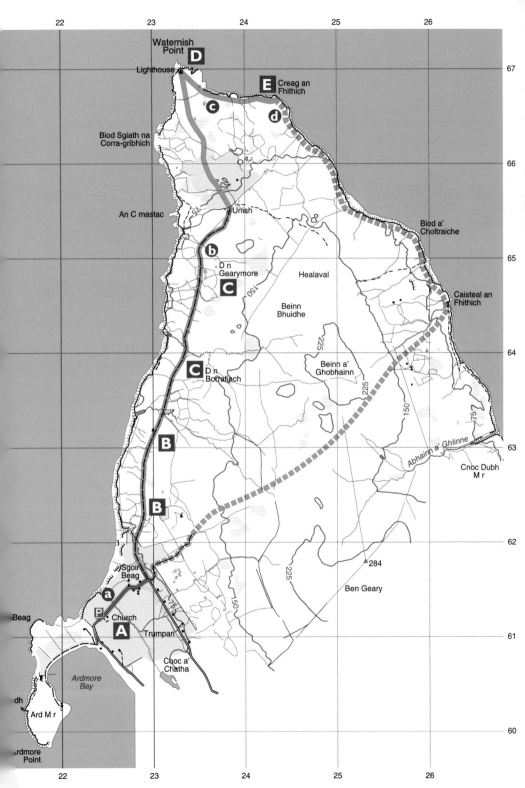

View east from Waternish Point to Creag an Fhithich

attempted landing further south at Ardmore had been abandoned when they were shot at by soldiers patrolling the shore. After their rest near the Point the party rowed across Loch Snizort to Kilbride.

c   East of Waternish Point the coast curves round a shallow bay on the far side of which rise the cliffs of Creag an Fhithich. There is no path other than sheep tracks but it is easy to walk round the coast.

E   Creag an Fhithich 244 667

Creag an Fhithich means the Raven's Crag and these birds may indeed be seen here, as they may around most cliffs on Skye. From the cliff top there are views south-east along the cliffs to Biod a'Choltraiche, which means Razorbill Cliff.

d   At Creag an Fhithich there are two options. The easier is to head inland back to Unish and the track to Trumpan.

For a longer and more arduous walk, though with compensating views, continue along the cliffs to Biod a'Choltraiche and then the sea stack of Caisteal an Fhithich (the Raven's Castle). From here head inland between the rather featureless summits of Beinn a'Ghobhainn and Ben Geary. On the cliffs the walking is mostly on short turf. It's when you turn inland that it becomes harder as the terrain is pathless boggy moorland. Initially aim for the south-east crags of Beinn a'Ghobhainn. Pass below these and cross the saddle between the two hills to pick up a track at 241 624 that leads back to the road and Trumpan Church.

BEINN AN SGUIRR

einn an Sguirr is a little known and secretive hill hidden in forestry plantations. There are excellent views from the summit ridge below which lie some disintegrating cliffs.

a The walk starts at the road end past the houses of Gillen. Go through a gate here onto a wide stony track that leads into conifer plantations. Keep straight on at a junction with an unsurfaced road made of packed stones that runs to a working quarry.

START/FINISH:
Gillen (266 599), which lies on the eastern side of Waternish. There is space to park a few hundred yards before the end of the minor road.

DISTANCE:
3½ miles (6km)

APPROXIMATE TIME:
2–4 hours

HIGHEST POINT:
720ft (220m)

MAP:
OS Landranger 23 North Skye

REFRESHMENTS:
Dunvegan

ADVICE:
The walk is on tracks and paths throughout. There are several unmarked junctions where care is needed to ensure the right turning is taken. Take care too near the edge of the cliffs as the terrain here is loose and crumbling. This walk could be done on the same day as Walk 2 Waternish Point as both lie in the same remote area.

Loch Losalt and Gillen from Beinn an Sguirr

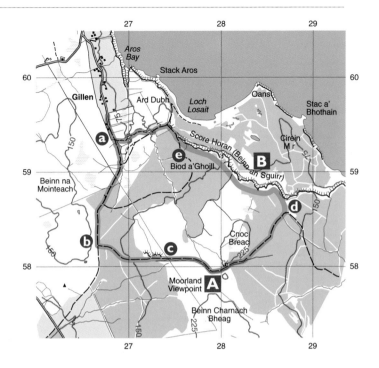

b After climbing slightly through a small section of forest the track runs along the western edge of the trees with open moorland to the right. Just before the track starts to descend to Waternish House you reach a junction (267 588). Turn left here onto another wide track.

Loch Losalt and Gillen from Beinn an Sguirr

c   The track climbs slowly up out of the forest to cross the broad moorland ridge running north from Beinn Charnach Bheag.

View across Loch Snizort to Trotternish from Beinn an Sguirr

A   Moorland Viewpoint 280 580

From the high point on the moors there are good views west to Dunvegan Head and the island of Isay and east to the long undulating Trotternish Ridge while away to the south can be seen the ragged outline of the Cuillin and the Red Hills.

d   The track now descends back into the forest, heading north-east. At an abrupt right turn a small cairn marks where a narrow path heads north (288 586) through a broad swathe of heather between two blocks of conifers. In a very short distance the edge of the Beinn an Sguirr cliffs is reached.

B   Beinn an Sguirr 282 591

Rather than a hilltop Beinn an Sguirr (also called Score Horan on OS Sheet 23) is a long ragged escarpment. To the north run the cliffs of eastern Waternish while out over the Ascrib Islands in Loch Snizort you can see Uig Bay and the Trotternish peninsula. The immediate scenery is impressive too. The rotten vegetated basalt cliffs are split by deep gullies

View east along the cliffs of
Beinn an Sguirr

and there are tottering ridges running out from the cliffs along
with more solid staircase-like blocky dykes of other types of
rock that have cut into the basalt. Below the rock landscape
disappears into more forestry.

e   Follow the narrow path as it winds along the top of the
cliffs. At times the trees run right up to the cliff edge and the
path cuts through the forest fringe. A slow descent starts
where birch trees can be seen on the steeper slopes below, a
burst of natural woodland in the midst of the plantations.
Soon the beach of little Loch Losait, really just a shallow bay,
comes into view. When the cliffs fade away keep the forest on
your left until a wide track running down to Loch Losait is
reached. Unless you want to visit the beach turn left here and
take the track back to where it joins the outward one from
Gillen.

GRESHORNISH POINT

Greshornish is a small promontory jutting out into broad Loch Snizort with Loch Greshornish to the east. It's a quiet place, a finger of rocky moorland edged with cliffs, that is ideal for a peaceful walk. There are many birds and the possibility of seeing seals and porpoise.

a At the bend in the road just beyond the Greshornish House Hotel go left through a gate and follow a track towards a beech wood. Keep left where the road forks and go through another gate onto a path that leads across the neck of the peninsula to Loch Diubaig.

A Loch Diubaig 332 544

At tiny Loch Diubaig (which means Loch of the Deep Bay) there is the first view of Loch Snizort, along which can be seen the Ascrib Islands, and the cliffs of the north-west coast of Greshornish. To the north-east the cliffs of Waternish disappear into the horizon.

START/FINISH:
The Greshornish House Hotel lies at the end of a minor road running north-east from the Portree to Dunvegan A850 road. A short distance beyond the hotel there is just room to carefully park at a bend in the road. There is no public transport to Greshornish.

DISTANCE:
3½ miles (6km)

APPROXIMATE TIME:
2–3 hours

HIGHEST POINT:
320ft (98m)

MAP:
OS Landranger 23 North Skye

REFRESHMENTS:
Dunvegan

ADVICE:
An easy walk suitable for an evening stroll.

View south along the Greshornish coast to Loch Diubaig

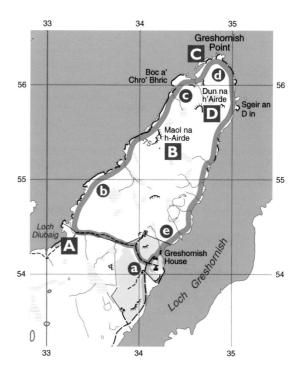

b   Head north-east along the undulating cliff top. The ground is mostly cropped turf, with patches of heather and the occasional boggy area, and there are many sheep tracks that can be followed. The cliffs aren't very high but they are steep so it's best to keep away from the edge. From various points caves and stacks can be seen below. Ahead rises the highest point on the peninsula, 320ft- (98m-) high Maol na h-Airde. Cliffs abut its western flanks so you have to climb it or at least pass close by the summit.

B   Maol na h-Airde 341 555

The craggy summit of Maol na h-Airde is an excellent viewpoint with the whole of Greshornish visible along with the Lyndale peninsula just across Loch Greshornish. There are extensive views across Loch Snizort to Trotternish too.

c   Beyond Maol na h-Airde follow further sheep tracks along the cliffs, now decreasing in height, to Greshornish Point.

C   Greshornish Point 349 564

At the Point a rich green flat area of moss and grass makes a good resting place from where you can look out over the low cliffs and broken rocks to the tip of Lyndale and tiny Eilean Mor and Eilean Beag (Big and Little Islands).

Greshornish comes from the Norse and means the Headland of the Pig.

d From the Point turn south along the coast of Loch Greshornish. There are still plenty of sheep tracks to follow.

D   Dun na h-Airde 350 558

Surrounded by the sea on three sides Dun na h-Airde, the Fort of the Height, is well protected from attack. Only ruins now remain.

e Continue along the cliffs until a farmhouse is reached. Go right of this to pick up a track that joins the outgoing one not far from the hotel.

Maol na h-Airde and the west Greshornish coast

Maol na h-Airde and the west
Greshornish coast

THE STRANGE SHEEP OF GRESHORNISH
Otta Swire tells a curious story of the sheep of Greshornish that
shows how easily inexplicable phenomena can be put down to
supernatural causes. Sheep were never grazed on Greshornish
because, it was said, the fairies would enchant them so they ran
round in circles until they died. In the mid-1800s the new owner
of the estate, Kenneth MacLeod, who didn't believe in fairies,
decided to investigate this mystery. One possible explanation
was that one of the plants growing on the peninsula was
poisonous. However when checked by experts in Edinburgh this
turned out not to be so. MacLeod put sheep out to graze and
they did indeed eventually run round in circles and die. 'Fairies',
said some locals. A few years later a botanist had a close look at
the plants once thought to be poisonous and found them
covered with tiny snails. Maybe it was the snails that were
poisonous. Again though this turned out not so. MacLeod tried
grazing more sheep with the same fatal results. This time he
took both dead sheep and the plants they'd been eating to
Edinburgh, determined to solve the puzzle. The experts looked
more closely this time and found microscopic creatures living in
the snail shells. The same creatures were found on the brains of
the dead sheep. It appeared they'd been breathed in by the
sheep. Once discovered the creatures were soon exterminated
and sheep now graze happily on Greshornish.

MOONEN BAY: THE HOE TO WATERSTEIN HEAD

The great curve of unbroken cliffs above Moonen Bay on the west coast of the Duirinish peninsula is one of the most spectacular coastlines on Skye. This walk crosses three high points – The Hoe, Ramasaig Cliff and Waterstein Head.

a From Ramasaig go through a gate onto a track that leads past some farm buildings and south across bleak moorland. Stay on the track to its high point at 395ft (120m) about 1½ miles (2km) from Ramasaig. Here you can turn south-west and climb the rough, boggy slopes to the summit of The Hoe. This ascent can be very wet after rain. A drier but longer alternative with more climbing is to stay on the track down to

START/FINISH:
Ramasaig. This is a remote house that lies at the end of a long single track road running south from Glendale, itself a long way west across Duirinish on a narrow road from Dunvegan. There is room to park in front of the house. There is no public transport in the area.

DISTANCE:
8 miles (13km)

APPROXIMATE TIME:
4–6 hours

HIGHEST POINT:
970ft (296m) Waterstein Head

MAP:
OS Landranger 23 North Skye

REFRESHMENTS:
Café in Glendale.

ADVICE:
A particularly fine walk on a clear evening as the sunset over Neist Point is spectacular. Care is needed near the cliff edges which are undercut and crumbling in many places. Because the road parallels the coast it is easy to shorten the walk if necessary.

Ramasaig Bay and the Hoe

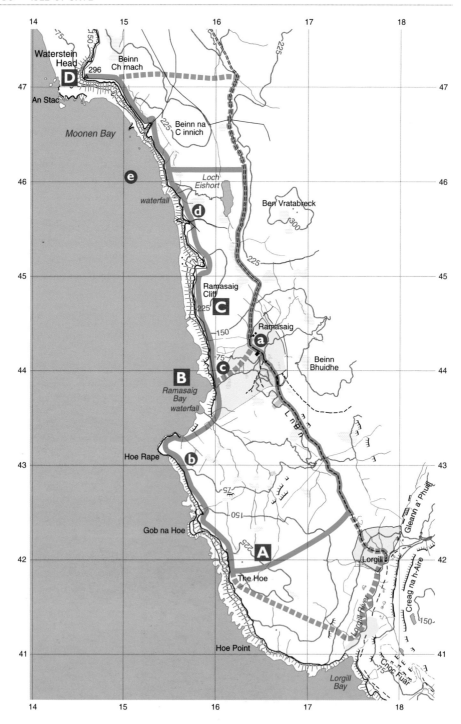

Lorgill (see Walk 12), descend to the shore and then go up the steep slopes of The Hoe.

A The Hoe 164 419

The Hoe is a rounded 764ft (233m) summit set back a little way from the edge of the cliffs. The views are superb and most of the walk to come can be seen with the great sweep of Moonen Bay leading past Ramasaig Cliff to Waterstein Head. Inland the flat-topped summits of MacLeod's Tables stand out while away to the south-east the distant but distinctive ragged Cuillin skyline attracts the eye.

b From The Hoe descend along the cliff top on sheep and rabbit cropped grass, a marvellous walk with splendid views throughout and many sea birds to watch – though watch out for fulmars in the breeding season as they can be quite aggressive, dive-bombing intruders. The walk leads over the headland of Hoe Rape and down to Ramasaig Bay.

Ramasaig Bay lies ⅓ mile (0.5km) or so from the start and the walk can be ended (or begun here) with an easy stroll on farm tracks through the old fields.

MOONEN BAY

Moonen is named for an ancient Celtic hero called Munan who is associated with Fingal or Finn mac Cumhaill and his warriors, the Feinne, as celebrated in the poetry of Ossian, Fingal's son.

Much more recently Gavin Maxwell, author of Ring of Bright Water, ran a shark fishery on the Isle of Soay and visited Moonen Bay to fish for basking sharks.

Ramasaig Bay and The Hoe from Ramasaig Cliff

Ramasaig Cliff

B   Ramasaig Bay 160 438

Ramasaig Bay is the only point on the walk where the beach can be reached. An attractive waterfall tumbles onto the rocky shore while just inland there are traces of 'lazybeds', an old method of cultivation. However the scene is dominated by the beautiful broad green sweep of turf that makes up the southern flank of Ramasaig Cliff. Ramasaig is derived from a Norse word and means Raven's Bay.

c   From Ramasaig Bay climb steeply up the greensward of Ramasaig Cliff following a fence. A barbed wire fence running crosswise to the cliffs has to be crossed. At the cliff end there is a short wooden section that is easy to climb over.

C   Ramasaig Cliff 158 450

240ft (787m) Ramasaig Cliff is perhaps the finest viewpoint on the walk as it lies between the other two high points. To the south you can see Ramasaig Bay and the cliffs rising gently to The Hoe. To the north an unbroken line of cliffs runs round Moonen Bay to the great prow of Waterstein Head. Jutting out beyond the head is the most westerly place on Skye, curving Neist Point with its lighthouse.

d The fence continues from Ramasaig Cliff all the way to Waterstein Head, making navigation simple. There are a few inlets where you have to divert inland a little way, as you do where the stream from Loch Eishort crashes down the cliffs in a waterfall. The walking is mostly on short grass.

D Waterstein Head 146 471

Waterstein Head is the second highest cliff on Skye at 970ft (296m), the only higher one being Biod an Athair at 1,027ft (313m) not far to the north near Dunvegan Head. From the top of the cliffs you can look back across Moonen Bay to Ramascaig Cliff and The Hoe and over Camas nan Sidhean (the Bay of the Fairy Knoll) to Neist Point.

e From Waterstein Head there are various ways back to the road and Ramasaig. Perhaps the easiest and quickest is to return south along the cliff edge until you are past Beinn na Coinnich then turn inland and cross the boggy moorland to reach the road just north of Loch Eishort. If you want to avoid the bog and the road altogether stay on the cliffs all the way back to Ramasaig Bay then walk up the fields to the road. The road can be reached most directly by walking east for 1 mile (1.5km) from Waterstein Head. However this leaves you 1½ miles (2.5km) from Ramasaig.

Dusk over Neist Point from Ramascaig Cliff

RUBH' AN DUNAIN

START/FINISH:
Glen Brittle. Highland Country bus from Portree via Sligachan twice a day from mid-May to the end of September.

DISTANCE:
7½ miles (12km)

APPROXIMATE TIME:
3½–5 hours

HIGHEST POINT:
165ft (50m)

MAP:
OS Outdoor Leisure 8 The Cuillin and Torridon Hills

REFRESHMENTS:
Small shop on Glen Brittle campsite. Bar with meals in Sligachan.

ADVICE:
An excellent walk for a fine summer evening. Often done when the weather is bad in the Cuillin but worth doing when clear as the views of the mountains are superb. The going can be very wet and muddy underfoot in places after rain.

The headland of Rubh'an Dunain lies at the tip of the peninsula separating Loch Brittle from Soay Sound. It's a relaxing place with fine views of the southern end of the Cuillin ridge and out over the sea to the islands of Rum and Canna. There are interesting historical and archaeological relics on the headland too. The walk to the headland runs along the eastern coast of loch Brittle, giving excellent views throughout.

A   Glen Brittle 409 206
Glen Brittle lies at the end of a long winding single-track road that runs from the B8009 near Carbost. There are tremendous views of the Cuillin ridge where the road crests the boggy

moorland ridge separating Glen Drynoch from Glen Brittle. Because of the proximity of the southern Cuillin Glen Brittle is a popular place with a youth hostel, climber's hut and campsite. Below the road end near the campsite lies the beach, a long strip of black sand popular with waders and other shore birds.

a   To reach the start of the walk go through the campsite and over the fence just past the toilet block. Turn right and follow a path past two water tanks. Higher up there is a 4WD track that can be used on the way back. The path stays close to the rocky coast and crosses several streams, the biggest being the Allt Coire Lagan, which drains one of the major Cuillin corries. There are some fine falls on this stream after heavy rain.

The Allt Coire Lagan can be difficult to cross unless the weather has been dry. If the water is high head upstream a

Coire Lagan and the Cuillin from the path above Loch Brittle

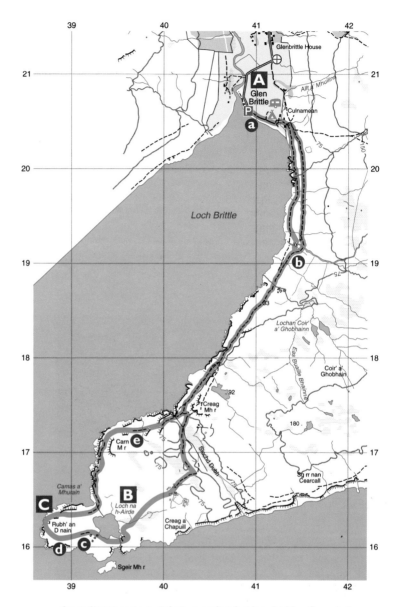

short distance to a rickety wooden bridge, hidden from below, that lies halfway between the path and the track. The path beyond the stream joins the track very shortly anyway so you might as well join the track nor far above the bridge. There are good views to cliffs on the far side of Loch Brittle and inland into Coire Lagan, backed by the serrated Cuillin skyline.

Rubh' an Dunain

b The track ends not far beyond the bridge, a narrower path continuing along the coast. This forks just below the small but steep crags of Creag Mhor. The left-hand path leads to the top of the crag, the right hand one continues along the coast. Either can be taken as both lead to a wall and the clear depression of the fault line of the Sloch Dubh (the Black Hollow) that runs right across the promontory. The path forks again here and again either can be taken to make a circuit of Rubh'an Dunain, the best way to see all the interesting features.

c Rubh'an Dunain is a tangled mass of boggy moorland, dense bracken and little heather covered knolls. Many paths – most of them sheep tracks – cover the peninsula. From the

View across Loch Brittle from
Rubh' an Dunain

Sloch Dubh take the clearest path, which heads south through a gap in the wall where there was once a gate. This path soon trends to the west and dwindles away. Continuing west the ruins of a large house come into view. This is Rhundunan, the family home of the MacAskills before they moved to Glenbrittle House. Not far beyond the house you reach Loch na h-Airde. All around are signs of old fields from the time when this land was cultivated.

B Loch na h-Airde 395 162
Loch na h-Airde (Loch of the Promontory) is an evocative place and it's worth taking a little time to explore its environs. It's rimmed with reed beds in places and is a haunt of water birds such as ducks and herons. On the south side the outlet to the sea has been deepened. Little is known about this though presumably it was made so boats could anchor in the safety of the loch. On a knoll above the channel there stands the ruined fortress or Dun after which Rubh'an Dunain – the Promontory of the Fort – is named.

Round the other side of the loch close to a wall lies is a shallow hollow in the side of a knoll. This is a chambered cairn dating from 3,000 to 4,500 BC. These structures were burial tombs and when it was excavated in 1932 human bones and Neolithic relics were found here along with pottery from the later 'Beaker' people (around 2,100 BC) who re-used chambered cairns. The Rubh an Dunain chambered tomb is reckoned the best preserved on Skye and is 11ft (3.4m) high. It was left open after the excavation.

Looking north-east across the loch there is a superb view of the southern end of the Cuillin ridge from Sgurr Dearg to Gars-bheinn with the pyramid of Sgurr Alasdair, the highest peak, in the centre.

d From the loch head west to the tip of the promontory then follow the coast round north then east to Camas a'Mhurain, the attractive little bay with a stony beach that lies north of Loch na h-Airde.

C Rubh'an Dunain 387 162

Low cliffs, spattered with bright yellow lichen, and a rocky shore mark the end of the promontory. There are caves here too. And much bird life, especially shags and cormorants which can be seen drying their wings out on the rocks. To the north lie the cliffs on the headland across Loch Brittle. The southern Cuillin look magnificent while Canna and Rum suddenly seem much closer.

e Follow the coastline round from Camas a'Mhurain to the Sloch Dubh where the outward path can be rejoined. At the Allt Coire Lagan it's easier to stay on the vehicle track for the return to Glen Brittle.

Loch na h-Airde and the southern Cuillin

SUISNISH AND BORERAIG

START/FINISH:
Camas Malag at the end of the minor road that leaves the Broadford to Elgol road at 594 201. There is a post bus along this road that may drop you at the start if you request this.

DISTANCE:
10 miles (17km)

APPROXIMATE TIME:
4½–6 hours

HIGHEST POINT:
525ft (160m)

MAP:
OS Outdoor Leisure 8 The Cuillin and Torridon Hills

REFRESHMENTS:
The nearest cafes are in Broadford, which has all amenities.

ADVICE:
This walk is mostly on easy terrain and good footpaths. However the route is unclear in a few places and the terrain can be very wet and muddy.

A blunt nose of moorland juts out between Loch Slapin and Loch Eishort. Two deserted villages, Suisnish and Boreraig, their people forced out during the Clearances of the mid-19th century, lie on the coast here. Also to be seen are sea cliffs, marble quarries, hut circles and other prehistoric relics and the beginnings of a new wood, the start of recovery from the depredations of the sheep that replaced the people. There is much to see and much exploration can be done away from the line of the walk at various points.

A Camas Malag 583 194

The shallow bay of Camas Malag has a pebble beach and a wonderful view over Loch Slapin to the steep rock buttresses of Bla Bheinn (see Walk 23) with Garbh-bheinn and Belig (see Walk 22) as supporting mountains. South of Bla Bheinn are the stepped terraces of Ben Meabost on the Strathaird peninsula. This fine scene is with you for the first 2½ miles (4km) of the walk along with the ocean and, away to the south, the hills of Rum.

a At end of the metalled road a wide track continues south above the coast, making for easy walking. Several burns are crossed including the Allt na Garbhlainn, Allt nan Leac and Allt a' Ghairuillt. The most attractive of these is perhaps the Allt Poll a' Bhainne as here a string of deciduous trees runs along the south side of the burn, a bright ribbon of green in the otherwise dull brown moorland. High on a rise just above

View across Loch Slapin to Bla Bheinn and Gars-bheinn from Camas Malag

the track and the burn is a pile of stones, marked on the map as a hut circle. Not far beyond the Allt Poll a'Bhainne the first walls and fields of Suisnish come into view.

On the track to Suisnish with the island of Rum on the horizon

B Suisnish 590 161

At Suisnish there are the remains of many houses, most just very low shattered stone walls, plus enclosed fields running down to the coast. It is surprising how green and cultivated the fields still look after 150 years or so of neglect. This is obviously good farming land. Just one house still has a roof (it was renovated early in the 20th century when an attempt was made to restart crofting here) though the doors and windows have gone and the interior is a mess of rubble and sheep dung. It is worth taking the time to wander round the ruins and follow the fields down to the coast and wonder what it was like when this was a remote crofting community long before any of the amenities we take for granted today.

Suisnish wasn't abandoned by its people. Rather, the people were abandoned by their laird, Lord MacDonald (and how ironic that title 'Lord', here signifying brutality rather than nobility), who had them evicted, or 'cleared', in 1853 and 1854 so he could graze sheep on the land. The people did not want to go so MacDonald had them forced out and their homes burnt so they could not return. Eyewitness accounts

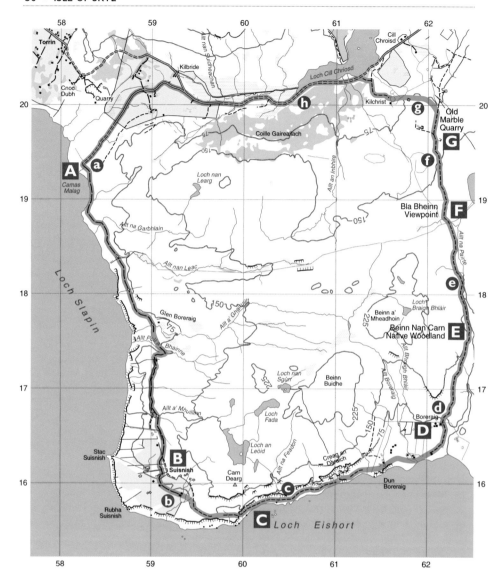

tell a harrowing tale of the evictions and the sorrow and desperation of the people. The remaining ruins and still green fields are a poignant reminder of this shameful period.

b The track winds through Suisnish to come to an end at a large green modern building, marked on the map as a sheep wash. Here cross a burn and angle across bracken covered slopes towards the coast on a narrow path to a gate. A good

path leads from the gate above broken sea cliffs of splintered rock and dirt. Inland rise the cliffs and scree slopes of 640ft- (195m-) Carn Dearg. As the gap between the two tiers of cliffs narrows the path winds down a break on the seaward side to the shore of Loch Eishort.

C   Loch Eishort 600 157

Loch Eishort runs between Sleat, the southern most part of Skye, and the region of Strath to the north. From the shore you can look across the loch to the whitewashed houses of the crofting townships of Ord and Tokavaig. To the east, beyond the undulating moorland of southern Skye, rise the mainland peaks, with the graceful cone of Beinn Sgritheall dominant. Oystercatchers call loudly from the beach and the air along with gulls and other shore birds. Seals may be seen bobbing in the water, watching curiously as you pass by. In summer the tattered pink flowers of ragged robin grow along the edge of the beach along with patches of yellow flag.

c   The path continues along or just above the beach, passing some waterfalls that are very attractive after heavy rain, until it comes out into the deserted fields of Boreraig.

D   Boreraig 616 162

The deserted village of Boreraig was cleared of its people for sheep at the same time as Suisnish. Again, the last low walls of the houses and the enclosed still fresh green fields are mute testimony to a destroyed community. Boreraig sits in a shallow green bowl surrounded by moorland slopes and ending on a stony beach. It's a quiet, secluded place.

On the cliffs between Suisnish
and Boreraig

There are remnants of older habitations at Boreraig. An old
dun or fort sits on a small headland overlooking the sea just
as you enter the village and there is a standing stone in the
middle of the fields.

d The standing stone, a fairly small slab of rock that is not
that noticeable until you are close by, is the key to finding the
way out of Boreraig. The walk leaves the coast here and turns
north, up onto the moorland that has edged the route so far.
A good path leads upwards from the stone into the glen of the
Allt na Pairte, a rushing hill stream. After about ½ mile

(800m) and at a height of around 375ft (115m) there is a stile over a fence across the path.

E Beinn Nan Carn Native Woodland 623 171

A notice by the stile announces that the fence marks the boundary of the Beinn Nan Carn Native Woodland, which was planted between January and May 2000. The new forest covers 680 acres (275 ha) and is 'designed to mimic native woodland distribution patterns which is essentially an intimate mosaic of trees and open space'. 240,000 trees have been planted, all grown from seed from native Skye woods. The species planted are birch, rowan, alder, willow, ash, oak, hazel, aspen and holly.

The absence of these native woods, and the need for fences if they are to return, is due to overgrazing by sheep (and also, to some extent, deer), which prevents any young trees from establishing themselves. The boggy moorland found over much of Skye is not the original landscape. Much of it is a degraded environment that could be restored to ecological health by schemes such as this one. It will be interesting to watch the development of this wood over the years.

e The path continues through the wood-to-be, following the burn upwards over wet, boggy ground to a shallow bealach. As this watershed between Strath Suardal and Loch Eishort is approached the pinkish bulk of Beinn na Caillich (see Walk 17) appears straight ahead to the north.

F Bla Bheinn Viewpoint 623 185

From the flat wet watershed just south-west of Loch Lonachan there is a startling and sudden dramatic view of Clach Glas and Bla Bheinn rising to the west. The mountains look massive, surprisingly huge, a disruption of the gentle and placid curves of the moorland.

f The path continues northwards from the watershed, descending slowly into Strath Suardal. The going is drier as limestone is the underlying rock here. Several paths appear, many of them sheep tracks. All will eventually take you down to the road but the most interesting route is on the main path as this leads to a disused marble quarry.

G The Old Marble Quarry 621 201

Marble is a metamorphic rock, limestone that has been transformed by extreme heat. Here the limestone lies next to a granite intrusion and it was the heat of this volcanic rock that turned it into marble. Skye marble, found mainly in the Strath area, is famous and has been quarried for many years. There is still a working quarry near Torrin, which is seen from the road near the start of this walk. The disused quarry you pass here closed in 1912. Tiers of rock, spoil heaps and large scattered boulders mark the old workings.

g Past the quarry the way can become quite confusing as many paths head off down the hillside. To shorten the road walk back to the start keep to the left (west) and head for the distinctive ruined house of Kilchrist, in the midst of another abandoned village. Pass this building on your right and follow paths down through the deciduous woodland of Coille Gaireallach to the road by shallow, reed-dotted Loch Cill Chriosd. The last name means Christ's Church or Cell and the ruined chapel it applies to lies not far to the east and can be visited when the walk is over.

h To finish the walk follow the road, watching carefully for traffic, west to the junction and the minor road to Camas Malag.

Descending to the shores of Loch Eishort between Suisnish and Boreraig

THE QUIRAING

The Quiraing is a fantastic maze of rock pinnacles and buttresses situated near the northern end of the long Trotternish peninsula on the eastern slopes of Meall na Suiramach. This walk explores the area then climbs the peaks of Sron Vourlinn and Meall na Suiramach. The walk to the Quiraing is popular but few people venture further.

a Across the road from the car park a narrow, exciting path winds round the hillside below a line of cliffs. Ahead can be seen contorted towers and pinnacles, the edge of the Quiraing. These are reached in just ½ mile (800m) from the road.

A The Quiraing 451 691

Despite lying on the side of a hill with views out over the sea the Quiraing is a secretive place, with a closed-in feel, because of the mass of rock features crammed into a small space. The first of these, to the right of the path, is a long narrow wedge of rock with a serrated crest known as the Prison. The seaward side of the Prison is made up of steep grass, the other side consists of vertical cliffs. Confident scramblers can ascend the Prison and even traverse its ridge but most walkers will be content just to look.

START/FINISH:
Car park at the high point of the Staffin-Uig road (440 679), the only road to cross the Trotternish Ridge. The Highland Country Portree-Flodigarry Circular bus service stops at Staffin but there is no public transport from there to the start of the walk.

DISTANCE:
5 miles (8km)

APPROXIMATE TIME:
3–6 hours

HIGHEST POINT:
1,780ft (543m)

MAP:
Harveys Superwalker Skye: Storr & Trotternish; OS Landranger 23 North Skye

REFRESHMENTS:
Café in Staffin, all facilities in Uig.

ADVICE:
Due to the multitude of paths navigation can be difficult in mist. The paths can be muddy and slippery too.

The Quiraing and Meall na Suiramach from the south

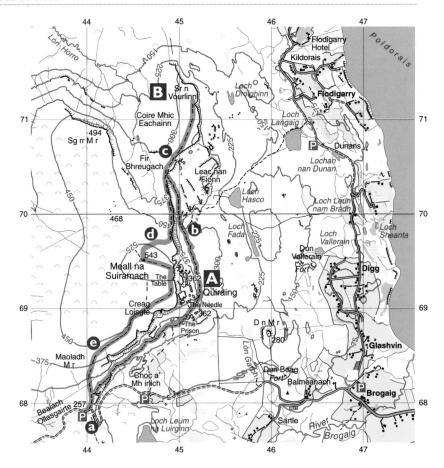

Uphill from the Prison is the Needle, a 120ft (36m) overhanging spire. This has been climbed. The SMC Rock and Ice Climbs Guide to Skye notes that 'the entire climb is on loose, rotten and dangerous rock' and that the ascent was 'recorded as more of a warning than as a recommendation'.

A path splits off from the main one here and passes behind the Needle, up a narrow gully and then between two rock buttresses to the heart of the Quiraing, a bizarre landscape of massed rock formations. Central to these is the Table, a massive flat-topped grassy knoll. There are various ways up the steep sides of this curiosity. The easiest are found on the landward side.

Behind the Quiraing rise the sheer cliffs of Meall na Suiramach. It is the collapse of this side of the hill in a series

of landslips that created the Quiraing. As on the Storr and elsewhere on the Trotternish Ridge the underlying sedimentary rock gave way under the weight of the basalt above, causing the latter to slide downhill, crumpling and folding as it did so. Water and ice, the forces of erosion, then did the rest.

The logical explanation for its formation cannot detract away from the strangeness of the Quiraing, especially when mist swirls round the spires and great rocks loom up suddenly in front of you. Surprisingly there are apparently no legends attached to the place. Otta F. Swire in her book 'Skye, The Island and Its Legends' suggests this is because something so horrible or wicked took place here that those who survived it, if any, never told their story. Having no legends attached to a place where you would expect there to be some makes it more mysterious than if there was a strange tale attached to it.

The most likely meaning of Quiraing is 'pillared enclosure', an

The Prison, a rock formation on the edge of the Quiraing

apt description, from the Gaelic 'cuith raing' according to Peter Drummond ('Scottish Hill and Mountain Names').

b   There is no way up the cliffs of Meall na Suiramach from the Quiraing. However the ridge can be reached further to the north by returning to the main path, left at the Needle, and following it along the base of the cliffs. There are good views ahead to Leac nan Fionn and Sron Vourlinn. Keep left here, ignoring paths running right. After about ½ mile (800m) the narrow, earthy path climbs steeply up a break in the rock walls to the ridge above.

c   On the ridge the ascent path connects with one running along the ridge. To the right is Sron Vourlinn, to the left Meall na Suiramach.

B   Sron Vourlinn 452 708

From where you reach the ridge it's only a short distance to the summit of Sron Vourlinn, the most northerly peak on the Trotternish Ridge. The walk along the edge of the cliffs is

In the heart of the Quiraing

wonderful with the great expanse of the island-dotted sea spread out to the north and east, a great contrast to the enclosed Quiraing. From the top you can see Rubha Hunish, the northernmost tip of Skye, and across Coire Mheac Eachainn to the cliffs of Sgurr Mor.

In the heart of the Quiraing

d Retrace your steps from Sron Vourlinn and follow the path along the edge of the cliffs of Meall na Suiramach, with good views down to the Quiraing and out over the sea. The 1,780ft- (543m-) summit of Meall na Suiramach, which has a trig point, is set back from the edge.

e The path descends gradually from Meall na Suiramach along the now broken cliff edge and over Maoladh Mor before dropping more steeply back to the road and the start of the walk.

THE STORR

START/FINISH:
Car park on the A855, 6 miles (10km) north of Portree. There is no public transport to the start.

DISTANCE:
3½ miles (6km)

APPROXIMATE TIME:
3–5 hours

HIGHEST POINT:
2,358ft (719m) The Storr

MAP:
Harveys Superwalker Skye: Storr & Trotternish; OS Landranger 23 North Skye

REFRESHMENTS:
Portree

ADVICE:
Navigation can be difficult in mist, especially beyond the Storr Sanctuary. Care should be taken near cliff edges as these are often unstable.

The Storr is the highest summit on the Trotternish Ridge and an excellent viewpoint. However the real glory of this walk lies in the shattered landslip below The Storr with its complex tangle of cliffs and pinnacles. Known as the Sanctuary this is a popular destination though few go on to the Storr itself.

a   The car park where the walk starts lies on the edge of a conifer plantation. Leave the car park at a gate in the forest fence where a notice informs you that the plantation is now owned by the local council and that the sitka spruce, lodgepole pine and larch are to be gradually replaced with native species such as birch, wych elm and hazel. There is

The Old Man of Storr rising above the other pinnacles of the Storr Sanctuary

The Needle in the Storr
Sanctuary

also a display about the Skye and Lochalsh Footpath Trust
who have rebuilt the once wet and muddy path through the
trees. It is now mostly dry (though it can be muddy in places
after heavy rain) as it winds upwards with occasional
glimpses of cliffs and pinnacles ahead.

A   Storr Cliffs Viewpoint 504 537

At the edge of the forest there is a startling view of the huge
cliffs of The Storr rising not far ahead. In front of the cliffs is
a tangle of pinnacles and other huge rocks though these are
not seen clearly until you are amongst them.

b   The well-worn path continues up the hillside from the
forest towards the highest of the pinnacles, known as the Old

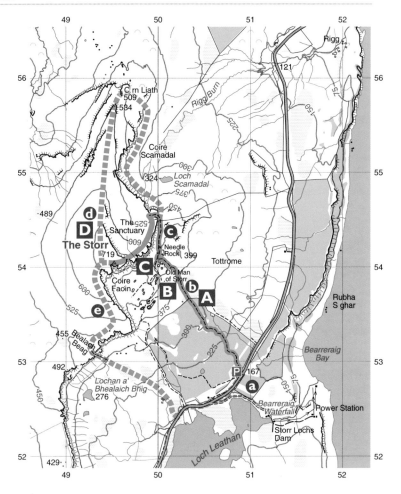

Man of Storr, which stands on a steep eroded knoll of rock, scree and grass. The easiest approach to the base of the Old Man is to the left.

B   The Old Man of Storr 500 540
This amazing obelisk is 165ft (50m) high and undercut all the way round the base so it bulges outwards, reaching 40ft (12m) in diameter. The rock is loose and friable but despite this the Old Man was first climbed in 1955 by one of the leading rock climbers of the day Don Whillans and other routes have been put up since.

C   The Sanctuary 499 541
Around the Old Man lies an area known as The Sanctuary. As

The Old Man of Storr

well as many tottering pinnacles there are great walls, towers and turrets of rock: an extraordinary collection of disintegrating stone. Near the Old Man is one of the most bizarre of these weird formations, a very thin wedge of rock, with two large holes in it where blocks have fallen out, known as both the Cathedral and the Needle.

The strange landscape of the Sanctuary is the result of huge landslides. These occurred because the thick basalt lavas that make up the cliffs of the Storr, and the rest of the Trotternish Ridge, rest on a weaker layer of sedimentary rock. The weight of the lava eventually caused the underlying rock to give way, resulting in the collapse of huge sections of hillside. The effects of weathering and erosion then carved the scenery we have now.

The Sanctuary is walled to the west by the 650ft- (200m-) cliffs of the Storr. A whole sequence of lava flows make up

View of the Storr Sanctuary from the Storr

these cliffs. At least 24 are visible according to geologist John L. Roberts in 'The Highland Geology Trail'. Deep gullies split the cliffs into a series of massive buttresses.

c After exploring the Sanctuary it is possible to climb the Storr by rounding the cliffs to the north via Coire Scamadal. Take the path that runs behind the Old Man and the Needle heading north below the cliffs. Cross a stile in a fence and continue below the now dwindling line of the cliffs. When the cliffs become little more than broken rock bands climb through them on a clear path and then follow the slope along the upper edge of the cliffs back towards the Storr, with some good views down the gullies that split the cliffs. The terrain in this upper bowl consists of scree, loose stones and patches of vegetation. It can be slippery when wet so care is needed on steeper sections and near the edge of the cliffs. At the top of the slope a steep grassy gully leads through the upper cliffs to the summit plateau. The triangulation point lies not far away.

D The Storr 495 540
At 2,358ft (719m) the Storr is the highest peak on the Trotternish Ridge, which can be seen extending in waves of stepped hills for miles to the north. There are distant views of

the Cuillin and of islands and sea too but perhaps the best views are those from the edge of the cliffs where you can, with care, look down onto the Sanctuary with the forest beyond and then the deep blue of Loch Leathan and the Sound of Raasay.

The word Storr is Norse and simply means a steep hill. It stands out in many views on Skye, its jagged western edge clearly seen from far to the south with the pinnacle of the Old Man prominent.

d   The quickest way back down is to retrace your steps to the Sanctuary and then through the forest to the road. However there are two slightly longer alternatives. The first is to head back north down the open slopes of the hill and out along the ridge leading to Carn Liath until the cliffs can be turned on grassy slopes. Then head south across a steep-sided corrie, on one shoulder of which lies Loch Scamadal, to rejoin the outward path from the Sanctuary.

e   The other option is to head south down steep slopes to where they ease off at the Bealach Beag. Descend from the bealach beside a small burn in a gully to pick up a path that leads across the boggy moor to the road.

The Storr cliffs from the summit of the Storr

BEN TIANAVAIG

START/FINISH:
Penifiler, at the end of a
single track road running
north from the B883 near its
junction with the A850 south
of Portree. There are regular
bus services to Portree from
Kyle of Lochalsh, Kyleakin,
Broadford and Armadale.
There is no bus service to the
start of the walk. There is
room to park along the road
at Penifiler.

DISTANCE:
3½ miles (6km)

APPROXIMATE TIME:
3–5 hours

HIGHEST POINT:
1,355ft (413m)

MAP:
OS Landranger 23 North Skye

REFRESHMENTS:
Portree

ADVICE:
Although short this walk is
on rough, sometimes pathless
terrain. Navigation can be
difficult in poor visibility.

Ben Tianavaig stands on a blunt peninsula to the south of Portree. Although small it's a beautiful and distinctive hill with a stepped profile visible from many parts of eastern Skye. The ascent is quite short and the views from the top excellent.

a   From the end of the road take a track eastwards and then a narrow path that leads over the stubby peninsula of Vriskaig Point and down through fragments of deciduous woodland to Camas Ban.

A   Camas Ban 492 424
Camas Ban is a small sandy bay with low cliffs at either end looking out onto the mouth of Portree Bay and the cliffs on the far side. The coarse sand of the beach is dark, almost black in colour, yet the name means White Bay.

b   Cross Camas Ban and take a clear path that leads up onto the cliffs and then runs along a grassy shelf. There are good views into Portree Harbour from here. The path then descends to a rougher, stonier beach where two small burns run into the sea. Big fins of rock project into the water and there are some small caves. Cormorants and other seabirds are common on the skerries out in the water.

The mouth of Portree Bay and the cliffs of Rubha h-Airde Glaise from Ben Tianavaig

Ben Tianavaig

c Leave the coast and climb the rough moorland slopes between the two streams. When the streams peter out continue upwards in the same direction to the summit. Low down the ground is boggy and there are patches of deep heather and bracken. Once high on the hill short cropped turf makes the walking easy.

B Ben Tianavaig

The summit, which has a trig point and a small cairn, is a superb viewpoint for the Isle of Raasay, which lies just off the coast. The prominent cone-shaped peak is Dun Carn, the highest point on Raasay. To the north-west Portree can be seen while northwards across Portree Bay the cliffs of Rubha na h-Airde Glaise and Sithean Cumhang stand out with the distinctive outline of the Storr prominent beyond them.

The round trig point sits on the edge of steep, broken crags below which lies a sloping grassy bowl containing pinnacles and other rock formations similar to those found in the Storr Sanctuary and the Quiraing. The formation of this landscape was the same as in these better known places, the upper basalt slopes slipping downhill when the underlying rock collapsed under its weight. When viewed from the south Ben

Tianavaig, with its even western flanks and stepped eastern slopes, mirrors the profiles of the bigger Trotternish hills to the north.

The name Tianavaig comes from the Norse and means peak of the bay, from tindar, a peak, and vik, a bay, according to Peter Drummond. The bay referred to is presumably Portree Bay to the north though there is a small bay named Tianavaig just to the south.

d To return to the start head directly down the north-western flank of the hill over increasingly boggy terrain. Where the slope eases off there is a line of small broken crags above Loch Meallachain. Stay above these for the easiest

Ben Tianavaig

descent, over wet moorland. The terrain below the crags is interesting but harder to negotiate as it consists of big tussocks and dense patches of deep heather and bracken. Below the crags there are woods of birch, rowan, willow and oak.

e Traversing Ben Tianavaig is a good option if transport can be arranged at each end. One way to do this is to descend along the line of cliffs south of the summit, which run right down to the sea at Tianavaig. Turn right here and follow the shore round to Camastianavaig and a road that leads to the B883.

f Alternatively, go north from the top along the crags until they end and you can turn south and descend into the bowl below the summit. Keep going south across the rough boulder strewn terrain and past a pinnacle. Soon the slopes start to steepen again and you can descend to the shore and follow it round to Camastianavaig.

MACLEOD'S TABLES

START/FINISH:
The road to Orbost where it crosses a minor stream at 256 444. There is no public transport.

DISTANCE:
6 miles (10km)

APPROXIMATE TIME:
4–6 hours

HIGHEST POINT:
1,600ft (489m) Healabhal Bheag

MAP:
OS Landranger 23 North Skye

REFRESHMENTS:
Dunvegan

ADVICE:
This walk is over rough pathless terrain. Navigation can be difficult in poor visibility.

MacLeod's Tables are two very distinctive flat-topped hills rising out of the rolling moorland of inland Duirinish. They can be seen clearly from many part of Skye and the view from the summits is excellent and extensive.

a The walk can be started anywhere on the single track road running south from the B884 to Orbost or on the B884 itself where it crosses the Osdale River (246 460). Which you

choose depends on whether you prefer a longer approach to the first hill or a longer walk back from the second. This description starts where the Orbost road crosses a burn, as there is room to park here and it seems reasonably central between the two hills.

From the road climb west a short way to cross a broad moorland ridge then descend slightly into Glen Osdale. Cross the glen and climb onto the east ridge of Healabhal Mhor.

b Ascend the steep, boggy ridge to the summit plateau. There are a couple of broken rock bands that can be skirted or scrambled over.

Dunvegan Castle, Loch Dunvegan and Macleod's Tables

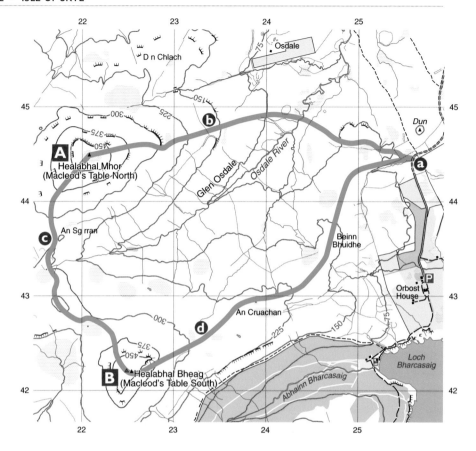

A   Healabhal Mhor 220 445

The summit of Healabhal Mhor is a broad slightly sloping plateau. The ground is boggy with few rocks so it's surprising how big the summit cairn is. This lies on the western side of the plateau. The view is superb though to appreciate it you need to walk round the edge of the plateau. Away from the edge the plateau itself cuts out some of the view. As you follow the edge the Cuillin, the islands of Eigg and Rum, the Outer Hebrides, Waterstein Head, Neist Point on the far side of Duirinish, Trotternish and Dun Caan on Raasay can all be seen.

At 1,538ft (469m) Healabhal Mhor is lower than Healabhal Bheag although 'mhor' means big and 'bheag' little. The reason is that Healabhal Mhor has a much larger summit plateau and so looks bigger from below. When the hills were named the exact heights weren't known (and were probably

Healabhal Mhor and Loch
Dunvegan

regarded as unimportant if considered at all) but the overall
size could easily be seen.

'Healabhal' is usually translated as flagstone, a reference to
the flat tops of these hills, and probably comes from the Norse
'hellyr' according to Peter Drummond (Scottish Hill and
Mountain Names). An alternative meaning is 'holy fell' from
the Norse 'helgi'. Drummond considers this unlikely as he
says the Vikings usually stuck to prosaic names. The legend
behind the holy fell name explains why the hills have such
large flat tops. According to this story when St Columba came
to Skye to convert the inhabitants to Christianity the hills had
pointed summits. The local chief did not favour Columba but
allowed him to preach a sermon after which he threw him out
of his fortress saying he would find no shelter on his land. As
he did so there was a huge roar and the earth shook and the
air filled with dust. When this cleared the summits of
Healabhal Mhor and Bheag had vanished, leaving the flat tops
we know now, created to be a bed and table for Columba.

The geological reason for the flat summits is that the layers of
basalt that cover Duirinish are horizontal here. The Tables are
the results of these layers slowly eroding away.

The English name, MacLeod's Tables, dates from the 16th
century and a visit by the chief of Clan MacLeod to King
James V in Edinburgh. At a magnificent banquet MacLeod,
provoked by taunts or boasts from mainland chiefs according
to some versions of the story, boasted that he had a larger
table, more impressive candlesticks and a more magnificent
banqueting hall on Skye. The challenge was taken up and

Macleod's Tables and Loch
Dunvegan

some time later some of those who had been at the Edinburgh
banquet, including possibly the King, came to Dunvegan.
MacLeod led them up onto Healabhal Mhor where a vast feast
was spread out on the plateau with a ring of men standing
round it holding flaming torches. Above the starry sky made
up the roof of MacLeod's banqueting hall. Happily it was a
clear dry night though whether the midges were biting the
story does not say.

c   Descend steeply from Healabhal Mhor south-west to a low
point called An Sgurran. The hillside is rough with small crags
in places though these can be easily bypassed. From An
Sgurran traverse a minor top and descend slightly to another
dip from where steep, mostly grassy slopes lead to the summit
of Healabhal Bheag.

B   Healabhal Bheag 225 422

Healabhal Bheag is slightly higher than Healabhal Mhor at
1,600ft (489m) but has a smaller summit plateau. It's still
table-like though. There's a trig point near the centre of the
plateau. However the highest point appears to be at the
south-west corner. Again there is an extensive view. Island-
dotted Loch Bracadale looks particularly impressive, the sea
reaching away south to the jagged Cuillin.

d   From the summit descend the steep north-east ridge. Not
far from the summit there is a very steep buttress. This can
be avoided on its left on a slope of loose soil, scree, rock and
grass. Once the steep top section is over there remains a long
slow descent over rough moorland to the little bump of Beinn
Bhuidhe and then the starting point.

SOUTH DUIRINISH COAST WALK

The South Duirinish Coast is perhaps the most spectacular and impressive coastline in the British Isles with high cliffs, sea stacks, natural arches, caves and waterfalls. Beyond these the sea stretches out to the Outer Hebrides. This walk follows the cliffs from the imposing sea stacks of MacLeod's Maidens below Idrigill Point to quiet Lorgill Bay. This is wild, beautiful country yet little visited beyond MacLeod's Maidens due to its remoteness.

a Beyond Orbost House an unsurfaced track runs down to Loch Bharcasaig, where there are good views across Loch Bracadale, then follows the shore round to some houses and the Abhainn Bharcasaig, which is crossed on a wooden bridge. The track now runs through a forestry plantation of mature spruce and larch to Forse Burn.

b Across the burn a cairn marks the start of a path. The walk follows this and not the track to the left. The path is narrow, stony and sometimes muddy but always clear as it climbs through new plantations to the bealach between Beinn na Moine and Beinn na Boineid. There is a good view from here of Rum and the Minginish cliffs around Rubha nan Clach.

c Descend from the bealach to a stile in a fence and a relocated stretch of path that avoids a muddy section. The path traverses above Brandarsaig Bay, passing the walls of an old shieling and new metal sheep pens. There's a little

START/FINISH:
Orbost House (257 431). Parking spaces on the verge just before the house; also the grass behind it. The walk can be finished at Ramasaig (164 444), or else retrace your steps or return to the start by an inland route. No public transport.

DISTANCE:
13 miles (22km) to Ramasaig. 18 miles (30km) for inland return to start. 21½ miles (36km) for return to start along the coast.

APPROXIMATE TIME:
8–10 hours to Ramasaig. 14–18 hours back to start.

HIGHEST POINT:
625ft (190m) for Ramasaig finish. 820ft (250m) for inland return to start.

MAP:
OS Landranger 23 North Skye

REFRESHMENTS:
Dunvegan

ADVICE:
A long route, through remote and rugged country. Good navigational skills needed, especially when returning by inland route. Much of the walk is pathless (despite the path marked on the OS map) and the terrain is very rough in places. Take care near cliff edges as these are often crumbling and may be overhanging.

Inbhir a'Gharraidh and MacLeod's Maidens

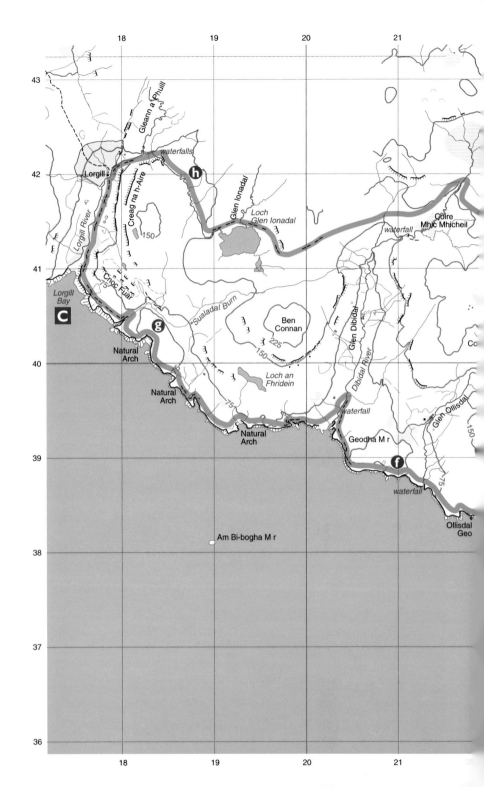

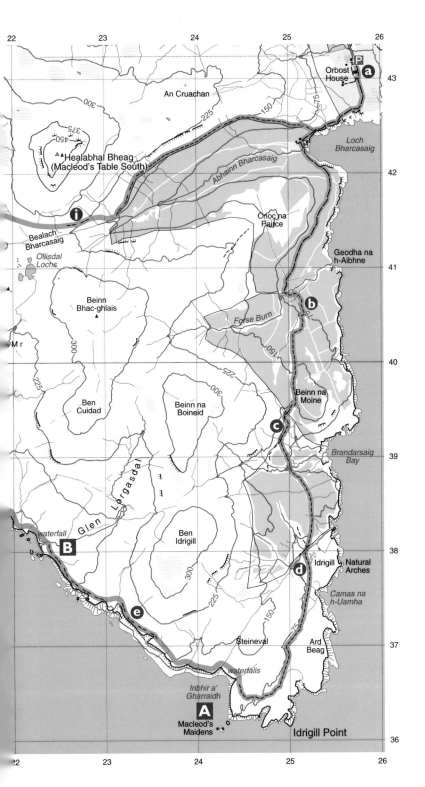

22 23 24 25 26

An Cruachan

Orbost
House P a 43

300 375 450 Healabhal Bheag
(Macleod's Table South)

75

Loch
Bharcasaig

Abhainn Bharcasaig 42

i Cnoc na
Pairce

Bealach
Bharcasaig

Ollisdal
Lochs Geodha na
h-Aibhne 41

M r Beinn
Bhac-ghlais Forse Burn b

300 150 40

225

225 Beinn na
Boineid 300 Beinn na
Moine c

Ben
Cuidad Brandarsaig
Bay 39

Glen Lorgasdal

waterfall B Ben
Idrigill Idrigill Natural
Arches 38

d

300 Camas na
h-Uamha

225 e 75 150 37

Steineval Ard
Beag

waterfalls

A Inbhir a'
Gharraidh

Macleod's
Maidens Idrigill Point 36

22 23 24 25 26

This is a superb walk for bird watchers as there is much bird life along this coast. Fulmars nest on the cliffs and can be seen flying close to them and landing on small ledges, often with a skirmish with near neighbours. Cormorants and shags hold out their wings to dry out on the skerries (rocky shoals just above the surface of the sea) and fly dark and low over the sea. Land birds may be seen too. Kestrels hover in the wind high above the cliff top turf and buzzards and ravens wheel around the headlands. Wheatears dart about on the grass, their distinctive clacking call attracting the attention. There are few mammals, other than the ubiquitous sheep and rabbits, though seals are likely to be seen bobbing about in the sea.

waterfall where the stream is crossed surrounded by a mass of rowans and a few aspen. The path continues on through the conifers to Idrigill Burn where the trees are left behind. Across the burn lie the ruins of a crofting village and some fine examples of the old lazybed method of cultivation – rows of raised earth on which crops were grown.

d   Beyond the ruins the path takes you through heather and bracken and over yellow tormentil dotted sheep and rabbit cropped turf between the low hills of Steineval and Ard Beag. There are many sheep tracks here and following the line of the original path becomes difficult. The walking is easy however so if the path is lost just head south to the coast and a sudden, wonderful view as the vast expanse of the sea and the sea stacks of MacLeod's Maidens appear.

View east along the South Duirinish cliffs to Macleod's Maidens

Lorgasdal Bay

A MacLeod's Maidens 243 362

MacLeod's Maidens are a group of three sea stacks near Idrigill Point. The largest stack and the nearest to the coast is said to be the Mother, the others being her Daughters. Otta Swire tells of an old story that the Valkyries of Norse mythology made their last appearance on Skye over Duirinish before disappearing, vanquished by the new religion of Christianity. The Valkyries were the 'Choosers of the Slain' who wove the web of death before a battle and then selected the finest of the dead and led them to Valhalla, the hall where they could feast with Odin for eternity. Sir Walter Scott called MacLeod's Maidens 'Choosers of the Slain'.

According to Swire in 1014 on the evening before Good Friday a farmer on the cliff top saw the Valkyries in the sky weaving their web. When finished they tore it in half and flew off north and south with the two pieces, 'denoting the rending of the ancient faith'.

This stretch of coast is obviously a hazard to shipping and Swire reports another legend that says that the largest Maiden is Ran, the wife of a minor Norse god called Oegir. Oegir was a storm bringer and ship wrecker. When their boats went down Ran would fish for the sailors whose spirits she then imprisoned. As punishment for this she and her attendant maidens were themselves made captive inside the sea stacks where they continue to draw ships to their doom.

The highest Maiden is 207ft (70m) tall and was first climbed in 1959. The climbers called their route 'The Old Lady'.

Sunset from the South Duirinish cliffs

You can look down on the Maidens from the cliff directly above them, though the crumbling edge is dangerous so you shouldn't go too close. The best view anyway is along the cliffs to the west, across the splendid bay of Iubhair a'Gharraidh.

e There now commences an exciting, breathtaking, marvellous walk along the cliffs. There is no path though there are many sheep tracks that can be followed and the walking is easy as it is mostly over smooth turf. From Iubhair a'Gharraidh the walk crosses the southern slopes of Ben Idrigill to a view right along the cliffs to The Hoe rising above Lorgill Bay (see Walk 5). Next comes a gradual descent into Glen Lorgasdal.

B   Glen Lorgasdal 222 380

The whole of the walk along the coast gives superb views but that from the cliffs at the foot of Glen Lorgasdal stands out. Below you there are sea stacks, pinnacles, a natural arch and a spectacular waterfall. The best view is back from the cliffs beyond the crossing of the Lorgasdal burn. Golden lichen covers some of the rocks and the strata are brightly coloured in places, making the cliffs glow in sunshine.

f Two more glens separated by headlands come next, Glen Ollisdal and Glen Dibidal. At the foot of the last the Dibidal River crashes to the sea in a fine waterfall. The glen is quite deep here and you need to take a traversing descent inland to cross it safely. Beyond Glen Dibidal there are many caves and arches along the coast. Seeing these is best done across from headlands rather than from above as the cliff top here is overhanging and crumbling in many places. From the stream draining Loch an Fhridhein you can see a huge deep arch in the next headland then soon afterwards a long tunnel-like arch is visible.

g The next descent is to the Scaladal Burn, which drops into a dark narrow arm of the sea in two long thin waterfalls. Ahead a massive cave can be seen in the cliffs. Above the waterfalls is a steep-sided gorge. To cross this go inland a little way then descend a path down to the burn and traverse out on a rather greasy rock ledge that leads to a good path. If you don't want to do this a few hundred yards further inland the burn is easy to cross where it makes a dogleg to the right. Once back on the cliffs after crossing the burn look back to see another long tunnel running through a section of cliff jutting into the sea. The steepest climb of the walk now takes you onto the final cliffs before the descent to Lorgill Bay.

C Lorgill Bay 174 410

Lorgill Bay is the first and only break in the cliffs on the whole walk from MacLeod's Maidens. It is a pleasant spot with a small stony beach backed by green meadows with a trickling burn running through them, a good place to relax after the drama and thrills of the cliff top. The history of the place is not pleasant though as there was a crofting community here, traces of which can be seen in the form of low walls and abandoned fields, who were evicted in 1830.

h The most interesting way back to the start is to retrace your steps along the cliffs. However this is also the longest route. If a pick-up has been arranged you can walk up Lorgill and take the track that leads north to the road end at Ramasaig (see Walk 5). If you've time to spare you could even continue straight onto Walk 5 and finish the walk at the road near Waterstein Head.

To return by the most direct route to the start head up Lorgill then follow the right hand branch of the burn out of the glen onto boggy tussocky moorland as it curves back south to Loch Glen Lonadal. Leave the burn just before the loch and walk

View along the South Duirinish
cliffs to the Hoe

east with the loch on your right then turn south and then east
again to the bealach between Ben Connan and Beinn an Loch.
From the bealach you can see across Glen Dibidal to Bealach
Bharcasaig, across which lies the final descent to Loch
Bharcasaig. To reach the bealach contour round the head of
Coire Mhic Mhicheil. To the north lies Healabhal Bheag (see
Walk 11), which is a massive block when viewed from the glen
but then becomes pointed when seen from the bealach. There
are waterfalls on the streams on its flanks.

i   From the bealach descend to the forest fence then follow
this round to the left below some steep craggy slopes to
eventually reach a narrow path, overgrown in places, that
leads down to the track beside Loch Bharcasaig and so back
to the start.

NORTH OF LOCH EYNORT

North of Loch Eynort is a little-visited area with a superb, exciting coastline of high cliffs and sea stacks. Inland there are some interesting hills that give excellent views of the surrounding area. This walk follows the coast to Talisker Point then returns by an inland route over Preshal Beg and Beinn Bhreac.

a   Loch Eynort is a narrow fjord-like sea loch. From the start of the walk the open sea isn't visible. Unfortunately the east side of the loch is marred by the extensive regimented conifer plantations of Glen Brittle Forest.

At the end of the road go through a gate and down to the beach. Take the path along the narrow strip of grass above the beach past the ruins of a church to the tiny Faolainn peninsula where there is a ruin and a somewhat dilapidated farm building. The path continues on grassy shelves above small crags and then descends to the beach again.

b   Just beyond Biod na Fionaich cliffs bar the route. The grassy slopes above are extremely steep here so it's best to climb the hillside before Biod na Fionaich is reached. Initially the ascent is on steep grass. Pass through a line of small low broken crags. Not far above lies a more solid line of small crags above a boulder slope. Ascend towards the right (north) side of these where they can be easily turned. Above the crags continue upwards across a grassy shelf to a higher one at

START/FINISH:
Loch Eynort at the end of the minor road from Carbost. There is a Highland Country bus service to Carbost but no public transport to the start of the walk.

DISTANCE:
11½ miles (19km)

APPROXIMATE TIME:
8–10 hours

HIGHEST POINT:
1,460ft (445m) Beinn Bhreac

MAP:
OS Landranger 32 South Skye

REFRESHMENTS:
Carbost

ADVICE:
This is a long walk over rough, pathless terrain. Navigation can be difficult in mist, especially away from the coast. If transport can be arranged the walk could finish at Talisker.

Stac a'Mheadais

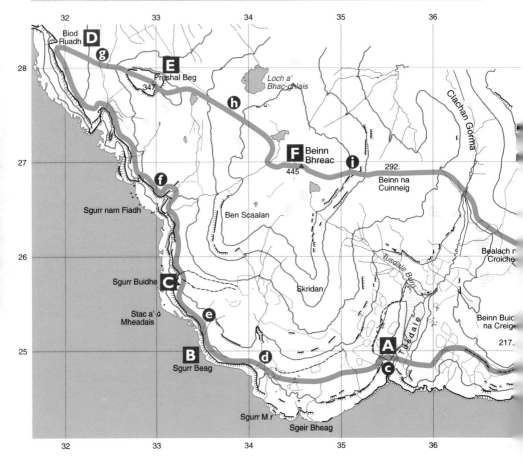

around 400ft (120m) where there is the first view of the mouth of Loch Eynort with far beyond it the dark line of the Outer Hebrides.

Follow the shelf round Biod na Fionaich above the cliffs then descend slightly to cross broad Tusdale.

A   Tusdale 356 249

The long raised mounds of old lazybeds and the remnants of walls show that Tusdale was once cultivated. Now sheep are the only crop. There are two waterfalls on Tusdale Burn, the larger upper one a lovely spread of cascades tumbling down a broad rock wall.

c   Tusdale Burn can be easily forded above the upper waterfall. However a solid stone wall lies on the far side. This

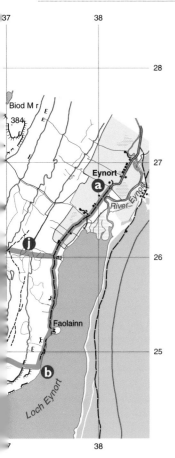

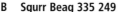

is mostly easily climbed at a right angle junction with another wall. Further upstream a fence replaces the wall.

From Tusdale continue round the coast high above the sea. As the cliffs lie below a very steep grassy slope you have to stay well above the edge. The next burn – unnamed on the map – lies in a gorge and you have to go upstream a little way to cross it.

d At Glen Caladale, a twisting steep-sided gorge, you have to go inland a little to a break in the steep walls. Once across the gorge you can walk along the cliff edge to Sgurr Beag.

View south along the cliffs to Stac a'Mheadais

B Sgurr Beag 335 249

From the little headland of Sgurr Beag you can see back across a shallow bay backed by huge 300ft- (90m-) high cliffs. Across the mouth of Loch Eynort lie more cliffs with Stac an Tuill, a sea stack with a hole right through it clearly visible. Ahead the cliffs continue with the squat flat-topped sea stack Stac a'Mheadais with its grassy cap below them.

e Beyond Sgurr Beag there is a superb walk along the cliffs with excellent views throughout. The terrain is mostly short grass and there are sheep tracks to follow. A fence runs along the cliff edge.

C Sgurr Buidhe 332 256

Just beyond Stac a'Mheadais lies the headland of Sgurr Buidhe with a curving cliff below it. From here runs a long unbroken line of cliffs. Standing out is huge Sgurr nam Fiadh, below which a grass and scree slope falls steeply to the sea, and the high sharp prow of Biod Ruadh. Much farther to the north the distinctive flat-topped MacLeod's Tables (Walk 11) come into view. Looking back a massive tall deep cave can be seen in the cliffs of Sgurr Beag.

Biod Ruadh and Sgurr nam
Fiadh

f The cliff top walk continues with the steep slopes of Ben Scaalan rising above you. As Sgurr nam Fiadh is approached a thin waterfall can be seen tumbling down the rocky slopes. To the north the sea stacks of MacLeod's Maidens (see Walk 12) come into view. The burn below Sgurr nam Fiadh is crossed beside a fence. Next angle up to the right to a break in the crags above and then follow the fence along the top of the cliffs. Inland the unusual crags of Preshal Beg make a change from the predominant featureless rolling moorland. As you pass this hill the climb begins to Biod Ruadh. The fence ends during this ascent.

D Biod Ruadh 319 283
Biod Ruadh is the highest cliff on this stretch of coast, its summit perched right on the edge of the 920ft- (280m-) drop. From this wonderful situation you can look back along the cliffs to Stac a'Mhadais and ahead down the descending line of cliffs to Talisker Point with a sea stack below it and Talisker Bay. Farther away MacLeod's Maidens, MacLeod's Tables, Dunvegan and the Trotternish Ridge can all be clearly seen.

g If you have arranged transport from Talisker you can descend along the cliff top to Talisker Point then turn inland to where you can descend to Talisker Bay and a track that leads to the road.

If returning to Eynort turn away from Biod Ruadh and the coast and head across boggy moorland to cliff-ringed Preshal Beg. The cliffs can be reached by ascending a scree and rubble slope to their base. A narrow terrace runs along below them that can be followed to where the slopes begin to disintegrate at the eastern end of the hill. Here you can climb up beside the last of the rocks then ascend rough stony slopes to the 1,138ft- (347m-) summit.

E   Preshal Beg 329 279

Preshal Beg is rimmed with cliffs on three sides. On the southern side these take the form of dramatic fluted hexagonal columns of basalt similar to those found at the Kilt Rock on the Trotternish coast, the famous Fingal's Cave on the island of Staffa and at the Giant's Causeway in Antrim in Ireland. These columns formed as the lava cooled. Above the columns is a very rough rock that is obviously a different type. Below the cliffs fallen pillars litter the ground.

The summit vista is extensive for such a small hill. Out to the west runs the long dark line of the Outer Hebrides. To the north-west the Duirinish coast stands out across Loch

Talisker Point from Biod Ruadh with Macleod's Tables on the horizon

Hexagonal columns on Preshel Beg

Bracadale with MacLeod's Maidens prominent and MacLeod's Tables rising inland with Loch Dunvegan and Dunvegan to their right. The long line of the Trotternish Ridge can be seen to the north-east with the Storr clearly visible. Bulky Glamaig rises to the east with the northern end of the Cuillin ridge to its right, the southern tops being hidden by Beinn Bhreac, whose bulk lies to the south-east. To the south Canna, Rum and Eigg are in view.

h From the summit descend just south of east over rocky slopes to a small lochan then climb the slopes of Beinn Bhreac to two lochans on a small plateau. During the ascent larger Loch a'Bhac-ghlais can be seen to the left. At the lochans turn south and cross boggy moorland to the trig point on Beinn Bhreac. The summit plateau is complex with many little knolls. A compass bearing is useful for finding the summit.

F   Beinn Bhreac 344 267
Beinn Bhreac is a boggy, mossy lump of a hill with an extensive summit plateau. At 1,460ft (445m) it's the highest point on the stubby peninsula between Lochs Eynort and Harport. From the top there are good views down Tusdale to Loch Eynort and over the sea to Rum. In other directions the broad plateau cuts out the views though the tops of the southern Cuillin ridge can be seen to the south-east.

i The eastern flanks of Beinn Bhreac are steep. To descend them head east from the trig point across the plateau to a lochan then north-east to slightly less steep slopes that lead to the spur of Beinn na Cuinneig. Across the long grassy glen of Clachan Gorma you can see the broad gap of the Bealach na Croiche between Biod Mor and Beinn Buidhe na Creige. A direct line to the bealach involves steep slopes and more descent than is necessary however. Instead head east into Clachan Gorma and across to the high fence that runs down the centre of it. Look for a ladder stile over this. Beyond the stile there is a gate in another fence running at right angles to the first one. Go through the gate then angle up to the Bealach na Crioche.

j   From the bealach descend steep, rough slopes to the ruined church just above Loch Eynort. Keep right of the church to find gates through the fences here. Once down follow the outward route back to the road end.

Hexagonal columns on Preshel Beg

CORUISK

START/FINISH:
Sligachan. There are places to
park just before the A850 road
crosses the bridge over the
River Sligachan. There are good
bus connections from Portree,
Broadford and Kyle of Lochalsh
with Citylink, Highland Country
and Skye-Ways. There are even
direct buses from Glasgow.

DISTANCE:
17 miles (28km)

APPROXIMATE TIME:
8–10 hours

HIGHEST POINT:
1,033ft (315m)

MAP:
Harveys Superwalker Skye: The
Cuillin

REFRESHMENTS:
The Sligachan Hotel

ADVICE:
This is a long walk to a very
remote loch. There is a
footpath the whole way but
the going is still rough and
rocky. It is also very wet in
places. After heavy rain burns
can rise rapidly, especially
around Loch Coruisk, and can
be difficult or impossible to
ford safely.

Coruisk in the heart of the Cuillin is one of the most dramatic, spectacular and beautiful places in any mountains anywhere. The approach down Glen Sligachan, although long, is the easiest way to reach Coruisk. The glen is impressive too, with the rounded Red Hills to the east and spiky Sgurr nan Gillean to the west.

A Sligachan 486 299

There is a classic, much-photographed view of the northern Cuillin from Sligachan. Dominating the view is the soaring pyramid of Sgurr nan Gillean (see Walk 27) with Am Basteir, the Basteir Tooth and Sgurr a'Bhasteir to its right. Between them lies Corrie Bhasteir.

To the east rises the huge cone of Glamaig (see Walk 20) while not far down Glen Sligachan lies the wedge of Marsco (see Walk 19).

At Sligachan there is a popular campsite and the Sligachan Hotel, which played a major part in the history of mountaineering in the Cuillin as most of the pioneers stayed here. There are many interesting old mountaineering photographs in the hotel that are well worth looking at.

a The path down Glen Sligachan starts on the east side of the road bridge. Just down from the car park and above the old bridge a gate leads through a fence. A signpost points the

Loch Coruisk and the Cuillin

Loch Coruisk and the Cuillin

way to Loch Coruisk. The path runs well above the river to avoid the wettest areas. However there are still many boggy areas and small burns that have to be crossed as well as the somewhat larger Allt na Measarroch. The undulating path passes a massive boulder graced with the name Clach na Craoibhe Chaoruinn about halfway to the low watershed between Loch Sligachan and Camas Fhionnairigh and the north and south coasts of Skye.

b The barely noticeable watershed is marked by two small lochans, the Lochan Dubhe, down to the right of the path. Just beyond the lochans and before the burn running out of Am Fraoch-choire is reached the path divides. The left-hand branch leads down Strath na Creitheach to Camasunary, the right-hand branch is our route to Coruisk. The path descends to the burn, angles across the wet upper reaches of Strath na Creitheach then climbs to a prominent cairn on the ridge of Druim Hain. Throughout the ascent the massive craggy west face of Bla Bheinn (see Walk 22) dominates the view.

B   Druim Hain 501 213
At the crest of 1,033ft- (315m-) Druim Hain there is the first view of Loch Coruisk and Loch Scavaig with the great curving

ELGOL BOAT TRIPS

A superb way to reach Coruisk is by boat from Elgol, an approach that has been used since the first tourists, who included Sir Walter Scott and the painter J.M.W. Turner, came here. Two companies run regular services on the boats the Bella Jane and the Kaylee Jane. These put you ashore at the landing stage in Loch na Cuilce. If you are returning by the same boat you have an hour to an hour and a half on shore, just long enough to walk a little way round Loch Coruisk. However you can arrange to return on a later boat if you want more time or even book a one way passage and either walk back along the coast, out to Sligachan via Druim Hain or over the Cuillin to Glen Brittle or Sligachan. The sea approach into Loch na Cuilce is awe-inspiring. As well as the mountains there are many sea birds such as gannets, terns, cormorants and shags plus the seals on the islands to see.

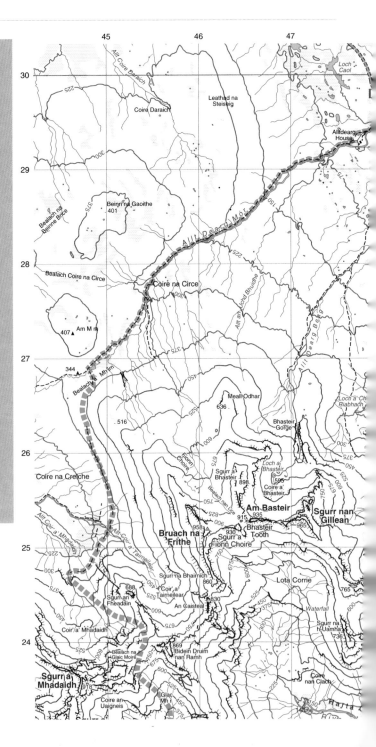

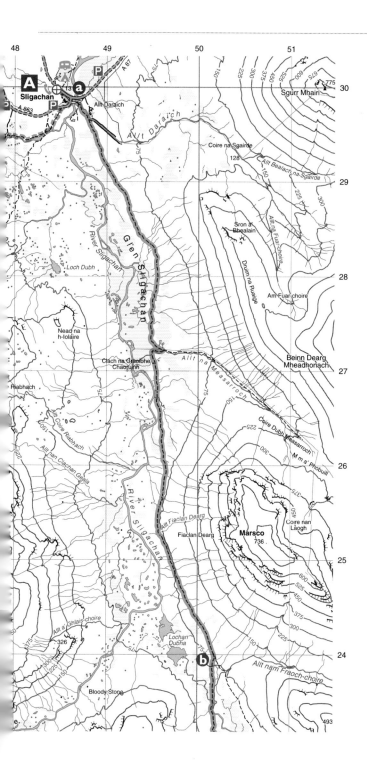

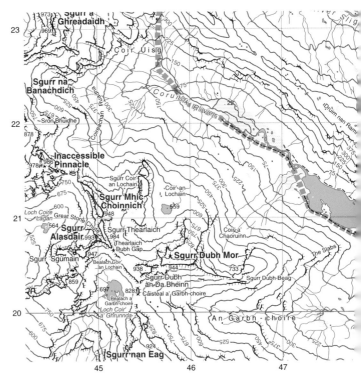

wall of the Cuillin rising beyond them. There is an even better view just a little way further on. Druim Hain is also where we leave the granite of Glen Sligachan behind and reach the much rougher, darker gabbro that is the reason the Cuillin is sometimes given the prefix Black.

Crossing the Scavaig River

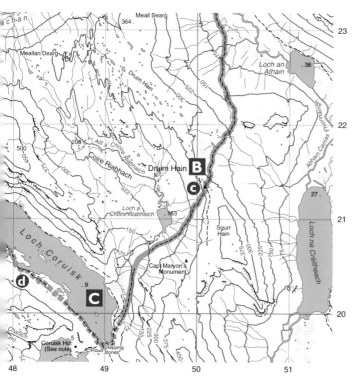

THE CUILLIN

The Cuillin are the finest mountains in the British Isles, a sensational sweep of rocky peaks situated on a long narrow ridge. The name is thought by most experts to derive from the Old Norse 'kjolen', meaning high rocks, a straightforward description like most Norse names. Peter Drummond lays out the arguments for this in his book Scottish Hill and Mountain Names. Drummond also gives 15 different spellings of the name that have been used at various times and points out that in Gaelic it is An Cuilfhionn or An Culthionn, The Cuillin. This is similar to the Gaelic word for holly, 'cuilionn', and it may be that this is how the Gaels interpreted the Norse word, likening the jagged outline of the Cuillin to the spiky edge of a holly leaf. In the late 19th and early 20th centuries holly was accepted as the meaning of Cuillin. Although widely used 'the Cuillins', 'the Cuillin Hills' and 'the Black Cuillin' are all incorrect and unnecessary. The range is simply the Cuillin. 'Black Cuillin' is particularly inaccurate as the rocks are not black but brown in a wide variety of shades and can glow gold and red at dusk or dawn.

c   The path runs left along Druim Hain a short distance then divides at another cairn. The left fork leads to Sgurr na Stri (see Walk 15). The right fork curves down across the upper slopes of Coire Riabhach before heading more directly downwards to the shore of Loch Coruisk. Below Loch a'Choire Riabhaich there are several paths, all of which descend to the loch. Some, especially those closest to the burn, run over steep slabs where a little scrambling is required. To avoid these slabs stay well left of the burn.

C   Loch Coruisk 492 198

Loch Coruisk is in a magnificent situation, set in a long deep hollow below the tremendous arc of the Cuillin. The rocks of the latter begin at the water's edge here and soar 3,000ft (915m) into the sky. Initially the view is quite overwhelming so great is the mass of crags, buttresses, slabs, ridges, hanging corries, spires and peaks that rise up before you. The north-east of the corrie is walled by the steep craggy slopes of long Druim nan Ramh (see Walk 24). At the head of the corrie are Sgurr a'Mhadaidh and Sgurr a'Ghreadaidh. From these peaks the Cuillin sweeps round to the south over Sgurr

Loch Coruisk and the Cuillin from Sgurr na Stri

na Banachdich (see Walk 28), Sgurr Dearg with the strange wedge of the Inaccessible Pinnacle prominent (see Walk 29), Sgurr Mhic Choinnich, the Dubhs Ridge, Sgurr nan Eag and Gars-bheinn (see Walk 26); an exciting, fantastic array of peaks. To see all this you need to walk along the north-east shore of the loch and into the corrie beyond. Indeed, a recommended excursion is to circumnavigate the loch. There is a rough, wet path the whole way.

Coruisk is an Anglicisation of Coir' Uisg, which means Corrie of Water, and as well as rock there is much water in the landscape with a myriad burns tumbling down the mountainsides into the loch. After heavy rain these burns rise rapidly and crash down in a series of slides and waterfalls. Coir'Uisg is usually used for the corrie beyond the loch,

Coruisk for the loch and as a general term for the whole corrie.

The loch is 1½ miles (2.5km) long and ⅓ mile (0.5km) wide. Its bottom is about 100ft (30m) below sea level. There are a number of islands in the loch and some sandy bays along the shore. Beyond the head of the loch the corrie continues almost the same distance again until it steepens into the cliffs of Sgurr a'Ghreadaidh.

Coruisk is a glacial corrie, carved by ice as were the peaks and ridges rising above it.

Coruisk is linked to the sea by the River Scavaig, at 1,313ft (400m) one of the world's shortest rivers. There are stepping-stones where the river leaves Loch Coruisk. All the water that enters Coruisk leaves by way of the River Scavaig and in heavy rain it can rise extremely rapidly, the stepping-stones vanishing under the water, and become impassable.

The River Scavaig runs down slabs into Loch na Cuilce, which is part of Loch Scavaig and a fine spot with a good view south to Rum. There are several small islands just offshore on which seals often congregate. A small landing stage on the shores of Loch na Cuilce is where boats from Elgol tie up (see Side Bar). On a knoll just above the loch is the Coruisk Memorial Hut, a private climbers' hut owned by the Junior Mountaineering Club of Scotland (JMCS). Just round the coast to the west a small burn, the Allt a'Chaoich, tumbles some 700ft (215m) down rocky slopes in a crashing series of falls into the sea. At least it's a small burn most of the time. In heavy rain it rapidly becomes a raging, foaming mass of white water, hence its other name of the Mad Burn.

d The easiest way to return to Sligachan is to retrace the outward route. An alternative is to follow the coast round to Camasunary and then walk up Strath na Creitheach to Glen Sligachan. This is a much longer walk however and much more difficult as it involves crossing the Bad Step, an easy scramble, where the cliffs of Sgurr na Stri reach the sea. A way back that is shorter in distance but will probably take longer is to cross the Cuillin at the lowest pass on the ridge, 2,493ft- (760m-) Bealach na Glaic Moire between Bidein Druim nan Ramh and Sgurr a'Mhadaidh, descend into Coir' a'Mhadaidh and then walk to the Bealach a'Mhaim and Sligachan. This is a very steep, rough walk that takes you deep into the heart of the Cuillin. The scenery is spectacular

Loch Scavaig, the Scavaig River, Loch Coruisk and the Southern Cuillin from Sgurr na Stri

but it is a serious undertaking requiring good route finding skills.

So dramatic are the Cuillin and so great is the effect they have on mountain lovers that people are wont to describe them in equally dramatic ways. The Himalayan mountaineer Frank Smythe said they were the only real mountain range in Britain while climber Ben Humble, author of The Cuillin of Skye, said 'they have no equal in all the world'. Humble's friend and mountaineering companion W.H. Murray wrote in Mountaineering in Scotland that when he first visited the Cuillin 'my wild dreams fell short of the wilder reality'. Hamish Brown sums it all up by describing the Cuillin as 'Valhalla, Mecca, the Ultimate …' (Hamish's Mountain Walk).

This wondrous world that captivates so many is the remnant of a huge volcano, all that is left of the chamber of molten rock known as magma that lay below the surface. This magma cooled slowly deep in the earth, crystallising into the very rough, coarse grained beautiful igneous rocks that make up the Cuillin. Gabbro is the commonest of these rocks. Reddish-brown peridotite is even coarser. Because of the roughness these rocks give amazing grip and are excellent for climbing. Intruded into the gabbro are narrow dykes of basalt and dolerite that cooled much faster than the gabbro, making them much finer grained. This means they are much smoother than gabbro and so more slippery, especially when wet. The areas of basalt are fairly small, though they do include the summit of Sgurr Alasdair (see Walk 30), the highest peak in the range, and the Inaccessible Pinnacle on Sgurr Dearg (see Walk 29). Even walkers with no interest in geology (a difficult feat in an area like the Cuillin) ought to learn how to distinguish between basalt and gabbro for safety's sake if nothing more.

Rocks like gabbro are rich in iron oxides, which makes them magnetic. Compasses are notorious for being unreliable in the Cuillin. This doesn't mean they are useless though but it should be taken into account. To minimise interference hold the compass at face height and take readings from a few different places. If these vary work out the average and use that.

Once the Cuillin must have been much higher than they are now. The current landscape is the result of glaciation, the ice carving out the corries and thinning the ridges to narrow aretes, and subsequent weathering. Basalt and dolerite erode at different rates to the gabbro, usually more quickly but sometimes more slowly, which is part of the reason for the extremely jagged nature of the Cuillin.

The main Cuillin ridge is a 7 mile- (12km-) horseshoe curving round Coir'Uisg and Harta Corrie. There are some 30 peaks on the ridge and its subsidiaries of which eleven are designated Munros (separate mountains over 3,000ft (915m) high). Much of the ridge takes the form of a narrow arete, a knife-edge in places, with the peaks, towers and spires as high points along it. Some of the summits can only be reached by rock climbers but many are accessible to scramblers and a few to walkers who don't like to use their hands.

To traverse the whole ridge is a mountaineering expedition. It was first completed in one day in 1911 by two climbers called Shadbolt and McClaren, who took 12 hours, 18 minutes. The current record is just over 3 hours 32 minutes, a time set separately by both Andy Hyslop and Martin Moran. To achieve this astonishing time requires soloing all the climbing sections and running much of the way.

SGURR NA STRI

Sgurr na Stri is an outlier of the Cuillin rising abruptly out of Loch Scavaig. It is a superb viewpoint for the Cuillin and Loch Coruisk, perhaps the best there is. This walk takes you along magnificent Glen Sligachan then up to the summit, down to beautiful Camasunary and back along Strath na Creitheach.

a Follow the route of Walk 14 as far as the crest of Druim Hain. Here keep left on the path that runs below Sgurr Hain. This leads past Captain Maryon's Cairn, a lofty monument marking where the missing captain's body was found, to a stream gully. Go up this gully until it peters out and then continue in the same direction onto the complex, rocky summit area of Sgurr na Stri.

A   Sgurr na Stri 500 193
The summit of Sgurr na Stri is a confusing tangle of rocky knolls. The two highest lie close to each other at the southern end of the summit. From the westerly one there is a sensational and breathtaking view of the Cuillin and down to Loch Coruisk. The whole ridge is spread out in a giant curve from Gars-bheinn to Sgurr nan Gillean. With binoculars you can study each summit in turn, marvelling at the complexity of the rock architecture. The eastern summit gives good views of Bla Bheinn and down to Camasunary but these don't compare to the view of Coruisk and the Cuillin.

Loch Coruisk and the Cuillin from Sgurr na Stri

Sgurr na Stri rises in a series of steep gabbro slabs and crags straight up from Loch Scavaig, blocking easy access to Loch Coruisk from the east. On three sides there are no walkers' routes to the summit. Sgurr na Stri is particularly impressive, appearing much bigger in relation to the other hills than it really is, from the sea to the south and from the coast between Camasunary and Elgol (see Walk 16).

Sgurr na Stri means Hill of Strife, apparently from a time when, according to Peter Drummond, the heirs to the chiefs of the MacLeod and MacKinnon clans were taken there to be told how important it was to maintain boundaries with neighbours in order to avoid disputes and strife. Drummond also points out an alternative rather more prosaic explanation for the name, which is that it refers to the buffeting of the peak by gusting winds.

b You can return to Sligachan by the outward route. There is an alternative though that visits Camasunary and lonely Strath na Creitheach. On leaving the summit keep to the right along the edge of the steep slopes above Camasunary. Follow the edge as it curves round the corrie lying between Sgurr na Stri and Sgurr Hain until the steepness eases off and you can descend into the corrie. In mist this could be quite difficult and it would be better to go back via Druim Hain.

Loch Coruisk and the Guillin from Sgurr na Stri

c Once down in the corrie descend to the Abhainn Camas Fhionnairigh and look for a safe place to ford this river. Once across follow the bank down to the sea.

B Camasunary 511 187

Camasunary is a beautiful bay with a sandy beach backed by a large expanse of smooth green turf. Sgurr na Stri rises up abruptly to the west. To the east the coast of the Strathaird peninsula runs out to Elgol (see Walk 16). Inland the view is dominated by Bla Bheinn (see Walk 22), whose south ridge soars to what appears from here to be a pointed summit. Directly up Srath na Creitheach lie two of the Red Hills, Marsco (see Walk 19) and Ruadh-stac. There are two buildings at Camasunary. One is a private house, the other an open bothy. Both are whitewashed and shine vividly in sunshine, a great contrast to the dark hills around them and the bright green of the grass.

The quickest way to reach a road from Camasunary is by the rough vehicle track that runs east for 2½ miles (4km) over Am Mam and down to the Broadford-Elgol road at Kilmarie. This

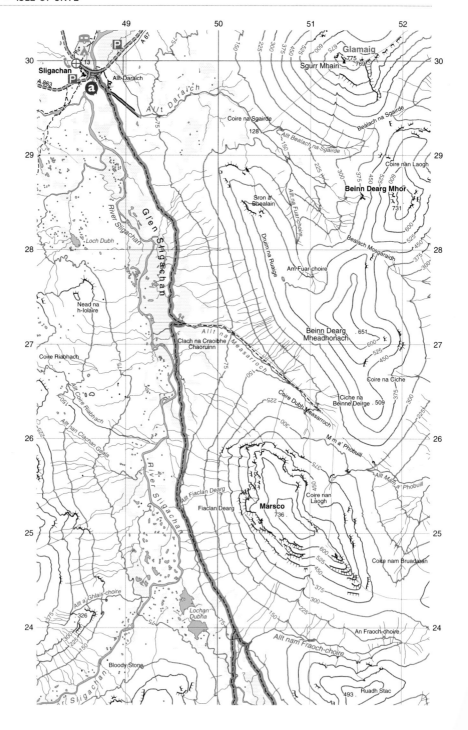

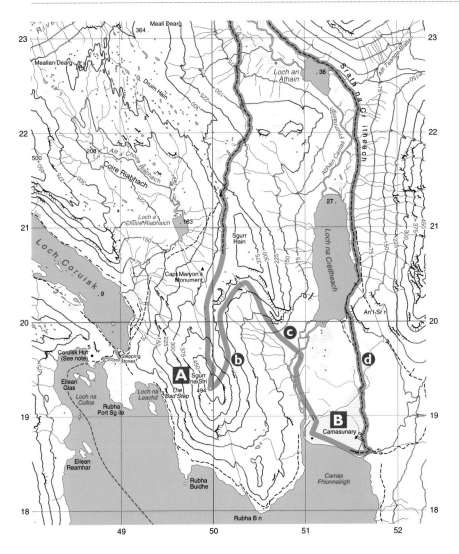

track is the last remnant of an unfortunate destructive
scheme dreamt up in 1968 by the county council and the
police to make access to Coruisk easier. As well as the track
suspension bridges were built over the Abhainn Camas
Fhionnairigh and the River Scavaig but the proposed blasting
away of the Bad Step, a short scramble on the route from
Camasunary to Coruisk, was prevented by opposition from
mountaineering and other outdoor groups. The bridge over
the Scavaig was washed away very soon after it was built. The
one at Camasunary was still just usable in the early 1980s

Camasunary from the descent
from Sgurr na Stri

but has since been removed with just the stumps of the supports left. The wildness and remoteness of Coruisk remains, as it should.

Camasunary means Bay of the White or Fair Shieling and is an Anglicisation of Camas Fhionnairigh.

d Walk along the beach to the east side of the bay past the bothy and the house and then along a path beside the bank of the Abhainn nan Leac for a few hundred yards to a junction. Here turn left, back towards the house. The right fork is the track over Am Mam. At the building the path turns north up Srath na Creitheach, soon reaching Loch na Creitheach, a long dark loch hemmed in by the steep rocky slopes of Sgurr Hain and Bla Bheinn. Ahead lies steep-sided Ruadh-stac, the pale pinkish granite slopes that give it its name (Red Stack) contrasting with the dark gabbro on either side. Ruadh-stac is the southernmost of the Western Red Hills. Beyond Loch na Creitheach the path continues up the glen to smaller Loch an Athain and then under Ruadh-stac and onto the junction with the Druim Hain path from where you can follow the outward path back to Sligachan.

THE ELGOL COAST WALK

The coastline between Elgol and Camasunary gives superb views over Loch Scavaig to the Cuillin as well as over the sea to the islands of Soay, Canna, Rum and Eigg. The path undulates below cliffs and along steep slopes, an exciting route into the hills. Camasunary is a fine destination, a beautiful bay under the towering slopes of Bla Bheinn. It is possible to continue further on a very rugged path with one scrambling section that leads to Coruisk in the heart of the Cuillin, a fantastic setting.

A Elgol 516 135

The small village of Elgol lies at the end of the long road running down the Strathaird peninsula from Broadford. It's an attractive place, set on steep slopes above the mouth of Loch Scavaig. The glory of Elgol lies though in the view across the loch to the Cuillin, a magnificent vista of soaring peaks rising out of the sea. Regular cruises run from Elgol to the head of Loch Scavaig not far from Loch Coruisk (see Walk 14).

The name Elgol is said to mean Holy Hill. Otta Swire gives a different possibility, telling of a tradition that the Saxon high king Vortigern sent the king Aella with a fleet to the Western Isles where he fought a battle with a united fleet of Picts and Scots at the mouth of Loch Scavaig. Aella was defeated but left his name as the first syllable of Elgol.

START/FINISH:
Elgol at the end of the road from Broadford along the Strathaird peninsula. There is a post bus to Elgol.

DISTANCE:
7½ miles (12km) round trip from Elgol, 10 miles (16km) round trip from Coruisk.

APPROXIMATE TIME:
3–5 hours to and from Elgol, 6–10 hours to and from Coruisk.

HIGHEST POINT:
330ft (100m)

MAP:
Harveys Superwalker Skye: The Cuillin; OS Outdoor Leisure 8 The Cuillin and Torridon Hills

REFRESHMENTS:
Elgol.

ADVICE:
This walk runs along a rugged coastline across steep slopes on a narrow often wet path. As far as Camasunary the walk is fairly easy. Beyond there it becomes much more rugged and difficult and takes the walker into very remote country. Just before Coruisk is reached the Bad Step, an easy scramble, has to be negotiated.

Camasunary Bothy and Bla Bheinn

Map reproduced at 85 per cent of normal size; 1 cm = 0.85km on the ground

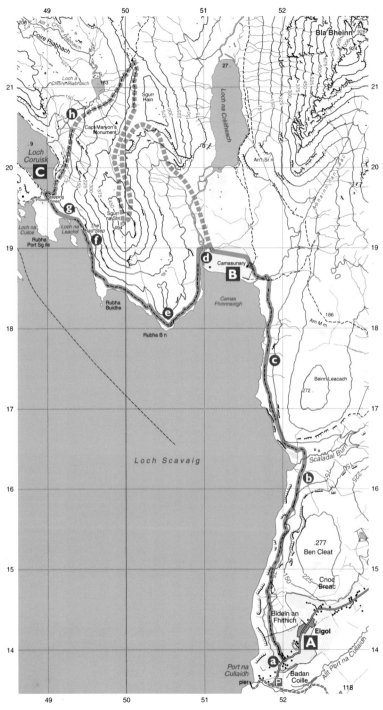

a The walk starts at a signpost on the steep road a few hundred yards above the upper of the two car parks in Elgol. A vehicle track leads past some houses to a path between fences that leads to the open hillside. The path traverses below Bidein an Fhithich (Peak of the Raven) then descends towards the coast. Next the path crosses the steep sloping hillside below the rugged slopes of Ben Cleat (Hill of the Rock or Cliff). The sea is now only a short distance below the path. On the north-western slopes of Ben Cleat is the rugged cliff of Carn Mor (Big Rocky Hill).

b Not far beyond Carn Mor the path descends to the meadows of Glen Scaladal between Beinn Leacach and Ben Cleat. Once across the Scaladal Burn the path climbs and enters a narrow strip of mixed woodland – aspen, oak, birch, holly and hazel – with steep vegetated drops to the sea below. There is a further scattering of trees above the headland of Rubha na h-Airighe Baine as the path runs across the lower slopes of Beinn Leacach (Hill of the Bare Rock).

Camasunary beach and the coast running south towards Elgol

c   Beyond Rubha na h-Airighe Baine the angle of the hillside eases off as the path continues on to the greensward and beach of Camasunary. At low tide you can cross the beach here and easily ford the spreading mouth of the Abhainn nan Leac. At high tide stay on the path to the bridge where the Camasunary to Kilmarie track is joined.

B   Camasunary 516 185

Camasunary – the Bay of the Fair Shieling – is a lovely, relaxing spot; a gentle haven in the midst of rugged, dramatic mountain scenery. (For more information see Walk 15). However here the nature of the walk changes. The relatively short distance between Camasunary and Coruisk – about 2½ miles (4km) – round the rugged base of Sgurr na Stri is over rocks and boulders. There is a path but you can't stride out along it. Compared with the walking to Camasunary progress is much slower. Some people will prefer to end the walk here and head back along the path to Elgol. If you do go onto Coruisk be aware that it is a long way back unless you are carrying shelter.

d   The first challenge beyond Camasunary is to ford the Abhainn Camas Fhionnairigh, which lies at the western end of the bay directly below the craggy slopes of Sgurr na Stri. The river is tidal to just above the remains of the old bridge and can be forded at low tide unless it is flowing very strongly. If it is too deep here go upstream a few hundred yards or more until a safe crossing place can be found.

e   Once across the river the path follows the coast just above the sea to the headland of Rubha Ban where Gars-bheinn at the southern end of the Cuillin ridge comes into view. Once round the headland more and more peaks appear and the terrain becomes even rougher and rockier. The path crosses the neck of the little peninsula running out to the headland of Rubha Buidhe then continues until it meets the barrier of the Bad Step.

f   The Bad Step is a huge boilerplate slab that runs down into the sea. To cross this involves an easy if somewhat exposed scramble. To reach the slab thread a way through and over some large boulders. The scramble starts at sea level where a wide crack slants steeply up the slab. Ascend this with your feet on the edge of the crack and your hands on the slab above for balance. About halfway up step left onto a small platform. Don't continue up the slab – that's the way to get into difficulties. Beyond the platform a narrow ledge leads across the rest of the slab.

g The path resumes on the far side of the Bad Step and leads round Loch na Leachd and across the neck of Rubha Port Sgaile between large rocks to arrive abruptly at the foot of Loch Coruisk.

C Loch Coruisk 492 198

The landscape around Loch Coruisk is perhaps the most dramatic and exciting in the British Isles. For details see Walk 14. There is an excellent walk right round the loch and other excursions can be made up some of the surrounding slopes. If returning to Elgol keep aware of the time though. It's a long way back. If on a through trip you can go over Druim Hain to Sligachan or perhaps cross the Cuillin at Bealach na Glaic Moire (for Sligachan) or Bealach Coire na Banachdich (for Glen Brittle), the easiest passes on the ridge. One exciting route I have followed a number of times is the ascent of incredibly rough An Garbh-choire to the Bealach a'Garbh-choire followed by a descent to Loch Coir' a'Ghrundda and the path to Glen Brittle (for details of this route from the Bealach a'Garbh-choire onwards see Walk 26).

h The route out is spectacular enough that there is no hardship in retracing your steps. However a good alternative, if there's time, is take the path north-east to Druim Hain and then climb Sgurr na Stri for the spectacular views of Coruisk and the Cuillin. From Sgurr na Stri follow Walk 15 down to Camasunary.

The Cuillin and Camasunary from the coast near Elgol. Gars-bheinn on the left, Sgurr na Stri just right of centre

WALK 17

THE COIRE GORM HORSESHOE

START/FINISH:
Coire-chat-achan (619 227) at the end of the minor road running south-west from the A87 just north west of Broadford. There is no public transport to the start though Broadford is well served with buses.

DISTANCE:
5 miles (8km)

APPROXIMATE TIME:
4–6 hours

HIGHEST POINT:
2,401ft (732m) Beinn na Caillich

MAP:
Harveys Superwalker Skye: The Cuillin

REFRESHMENTS:
Broadford

ADVICE:
Although short this is a rough, steep walk over stony hills. There is no path so good navigational skills are required. There is no water on most of the route so full bottles should be carried, especially in hot weather.

The massive rounded bulk of Beinn na Caillich towers over Broadford, making it very much Broadford's hill. It is the easternmost of the granite Red Hills. The ascent up steep slopes over bog, scree and rock is arduous but the view from the top is excellent and the ridge walk over Beinn Dearg Mhor and Beinn Dearg Bheag round the head of Coire Gorm (Blue Corrie) is very enjoyable. If you prefer a gentler ascent at the start of the day then this walk can be done the other way round.

A Coire-chat-achan 621 227

The ruins of Coire-chat-achan are the remnants of an old house belonging to the MacKinnon clan. Thomas Pennant stayed here before ascending Beinn na Caillich in 1772, the first recorded ascent of any hill on Skye. In his book 'Voyage to the Hebrides' Pennant described the view west to the Red Hills and the Cuillin as 'desolation itself; a savage series of rude mountains, discoloured, black and red, as if by the rage of fire'. Samuel Johnson and James Boswell stayed in the house a year later during their tour of the Hebrides, Johnson noting that 'the hill behind the house we did not climb'. Others did though and in the early 1800s Beinn na Caillich became the most climbed hill on Skye at a time when the Cuillin were unclimbed and few even attempted to ascend any of the summits.

Beinn na Caillich rising above Broadford

The Coire Gorm Horseshoe.
From the left: Beinn na Caillich,
Beinn Dearg Mhor and Beinn
Dearg Rheag

Coire-chat-achan is the Corrie of the Wild Cats and said to be the last stronghold of these animals before their extermination on Skye. Whether they have actually been exterminated is open to question. The Yoxons report recent sightings of possible wild cats in their booklet Wildlife of Skye and Raasay.

a   A small burn lies just west of the road end. Follow this burn up over the initial boggy slopes where there is a mix of heather, bracken, bog asphodel, bog cotton, reeds and, in season, orchids. Where the burn runs through a little rocky gorge alder, birch, rowan and holly grow on its slopes, showing that this moor would be at least sparsely wooded but for overgrazing. There are very intermittent rough paths on both sides of the burn. When the burn peters out head for the right hand skyline, which is the rim of Coire Fearchair. The way ahead looks very steep but the view is foreshortened and it's easier than it appears.

b   At around 800ft (250m) the boulders and scree begin. From here to the top is very stony underfoot. There are patches of heather but boulder hopping on the rocks is generally easier as at least you can see the terrain while the vegetation hides holes and rocks. There are bits of path throughout the ascent. In places there is some optional scrambling on rough granite slabs. As this is a convex slope the summit cannot be seen until you are very close. As you approach it grass starts to appear and the going is easier. Then the huge summit cairn and the trig point come into view and the climbing is over.

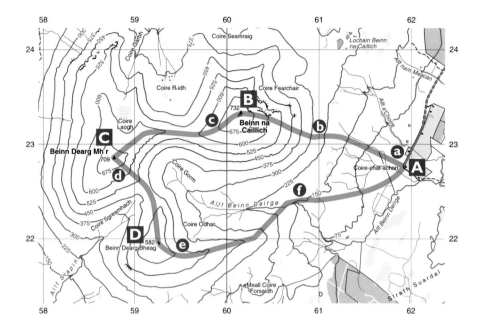

B   Beinn na Caillich 602 233

The summit of 2,401ft (732m) Beinn na Caillich is a marvellous viewpoint, perhaps the best of the high peaks for views of the mainland hills due to its easterly situation. A whole sweep of peaks from Torridon and Applecross south is visible but the one that stands out is shapely Beinn Sgritheall above Glenelg. Much closer to, Broadford Bay, lying almost below your feet, looks tremendous. Off the coast you can see the islands of Raasay, Scalpay and Pabay. Further round to the north the profile of the Storr can be seen on distant Trotternish. However the most stupendous vista is that to the west where Bla Bheinn, the Red Hills and the Cuillin look tremendous, a tangle of rock and scree in a multitude of shapes from rounded domes to sharp pinnacles.

Beinn na Caillich means Hill of the Old Woman. There is a legend that the huge summit cairn was erected over the body of a homesick Norwegian princess who asked to be buried up here so that the cold north winds of Norway could sweep over here or, in another version, so that she could look out to her homeland. The existence of the cairn shows that people climbed this hill long before Pennant thought of doing so.

The great scree and rock pyramid of Beinn na Caillich dominates many of the views in southern Skye, especially along the coast road from Kyleakin to Strollamus.

Beinn na Caillich and Beinn Dearg Mhor

Beinn na Caillich is classified in Scottish mountain lists as a Graham, that is a summit between 2,000 and 2,500ft (610–762m).

c From the summit descend the steep grass, scree and rock slopes of the west ridge of Beinn na Caillich to a bealach. A narrower ridge heads upward between the steep walls of Coire Reidh and Coire Gorm and curves round the back of the latter to the summit of Beinn Dearg Mhor.

C   Beinn Dearg Mhor 588 229
2,325ft- (709m-) Beinn Dearg Mhor lies at the apex of the Coire Gorm Horseshoe. The summit has a large cairn and an impressive view, especially of the long rugged east face of Bla Bheinn along with Clach Glas, Garbh-bheinn and Belig, a great wall of rock rising above the waters of Loch Slapin.

The name means Big Red Hill, a reference to the pink colour of the granite the hill is made from.

d The summit of Beinn Dearg Mhor is extensive and care has to be taken to find the right route down to the bealach with Beinn Dearg Mhor as the ridge leading to it is not distinct at the top. In mist careful navigation is required. The descent is on very steep loose scree. There is a slippery path in places but this doesn't actually help much. From the bealach a short ascent leads to yet another large cairn, this time on the third and last summit of the horseshoe, Beinn Dearg Bheag.

THE RED HILLS

The Red Hills are a range of rounded, steep-sided hills lying east and slightly north of the Cuillin. Their bulky slopes dominate the landscape between Broadford and Sligachan, forcing the coast road to wind round them. There are two groups of Red Hills, the Eastern Red Hills between Loch Ainort and Broadford, which include Beinn na Caillich, and the Western Red Hills, which form the eastern side of Glen Sligachan.

The name comes from the Gaelic 'Na Beinnean Dearga' and is a local description. It's sometimes given as the Red Cuillin rather than the Red Hills with the Cuillin themselves called the Black Cuillin, though this last was apparently never a local Gaelic name. Indeed, as Peter Drummond points out in Scottish Hill and Mountain Names, the Cuillin has a Red Hill of its own (Sgurr Dearg) plus a yellow nose or shoulder (Sron Bhuidhe).

The reason for the name lies in the pale pink colour of the granite that makes up these hills, a great contrast to the dark rocks of the Cuillin. Vast screes cover the sides of many of the Red Hills but there are few cliffs or large rocks and the summits are rounded and often grassy.

Like the Cuillin the Red Hills are the remnants of large volcanoes. Granite is a coarse-grained igneous rock with many large crystals. The volcanic activity that resulted in the Red Hills took place later than that which formed the Cuillin and there were very few intrusions of other rocks. This allowed for more even weathering of the hills, resulting in the smooth, rounded slopes and summits.

Because the Cuillin are so spectacular the Red Hills are often overlooked. Yet they are a fine range in their own right and especially suited to the walker who doesn't want to undertake scrambling or wandering along knife edge ridges over big drops.

D Beinn Dearg Bheag 593 219
At 1,909ft (582m) Beinn Dearg Bheag (Little Red Hill) is
much lower than the other two summits of the horseshoe. The
view is still excellent however, especially south over the sea
to the islands of Rum and Eigg. Bla Bheinn is still impressive
but most of the Cuillin is hidden behind it with just the peaks
at either end of the ridge, Gars-bheinn and Sgurr nan Gillean,
visible.

e From the summit descend the curving ridge round Coire
Odhair. This becomes the east ridge, which leads down to the
Allt Beinn Deirge, the first water on the walk since the burn
on the lower slopes of Beinn na Caillich. There is a good view
into the heart of Coire Gorm from the burn. During the
descent the scree and rock of the mountains is finally left
behind for boggy moorland.

f Cross the Allt Beinn Deirge, then head over the rough
moor back to Coire-chat-achan with a view ahead to
Broadford Bay, the island of Pabay and the Inner Sound.

Beinn na Caillach and Beinn
Dearg Mhor from Marsco

THE TROTTERNISH RIDGE

START/FINISH:
Duntulm, on the A855. (414 741). Highland Country's Portree-Flodigarry Circular bus service stops at Duntulm Hotel. Several services a day from late May to end Sept. Walk ends in Portree.

DISTANCE:
22 miles (37km)

APPROXIMATE TIME:
14–20 hours; can split over 2 days.

HIGHEST POINT:
2,358ft (719m) The Storr

MAP:
Harveys Superwalker Skye: Storr & Trotternish; OS Landranger 23 North Skye

REFRESHMENTS:
Duntulm Hotel at the start and in Portree at the end if you arrive before all is closed!

ADVICE:
A very long walk, mostly over pathless terrain. One road crosses the route, so it is a serious under-taking. Can be done over 2 days, with an intermediate camp; many superb places to camp along the way. In mist, good navigational skills are required. The eastern edge of the ridge is lined with cliffs, care is needed near these. Little shelter in storms. Escaping from the ridge involves a long walk over rough terrain both to east or west, with transport problems on reaching the road. The easiest way to do the walk is to catch the bus to Duntulm and to walk back to Portree.

The Trotternish Ridge is a magnificent high level escarpment running along the spine of the Trotternish peninsula. A series of cliffs, pinnacles, towers and other rock landforms decorate the eastern slopes, the result of a series of landslides. Some 15 miles (24km) in length this is by far the longest ridge on Skye and the walk along the crest of it is one of the finest excursions on the island. Much of the walking is on sheep-cropped turf and there are superb views throughout, especially of the ridge itself and the sea to either side. In the description below I have singled out just a few of the many viewpoints but it is worth pausing on all the summits.

a The walk starts on the A855 near the Duntulm Hotel. Begin by walking walk east along the A855 past Cnoc Roll, a little hill with a communications mast on its summit, then turn down a minor road that runs along the east side of the hill. Follow this road above some houses to the edge of the open moor where it becomes a rough track. Ahead rise Sgurr Mor and Sron Vourlinn, the northernmost summits on the ridge. Take the track across the moor and up a small slope to where it peters out.

If you have transport a little distance can be cut from the route by starting at the end of the minor road to Connista (426 732) from where you head over the moor to Glen Scamadal.

Sron Vourlinn and Sgurr Mor at the northern end of the Trotternish Ridge

b   From the end of the track head across the boggy moor towards the ravine of Glen Scamadal, a distinctive rift in the steep slopes of Sgurr Mor. There is no path. The Kilmaluag River has to be forded. This stream swirls slowly in deep pools in places but there are shallow sections where it runs over stones. If necessary go upstream in search of one of these. Once over the river head again for Glen Scamadal. As the terrain begins to steepen climb the slopes to the left of the gorge and curve left onto the gentle, rounded summit of Sgurr Mor. There is no cairn on the grassy top. Looking back you can see Meall Tuath and the northernmost coast of Skye. Ahead lies Meall na Suiramach, an easy walk over mostly grassy ground.

Sron Vourlinn from the slopes of Meall na Suiramach

c   On Meall Suiramach the last part of the route described in Walk 8 is joined. The trig point is set back from the cliffs. However the best views are from the cliff edge where you can look down on the shattered landscape of the Quiraing (see Walk 8 for details). The edge is then followed to Maoladh Mor from where steep slopes lead down to the Staffin-Uig road, the only one to cross the ridge. On the descent there are excellent views ahead to the next summit, Biode Buidhe, with the crag-

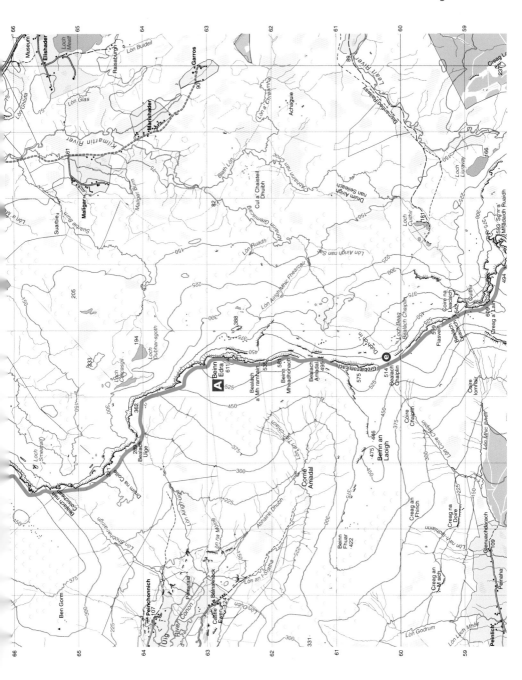

Map reproduced at 70 per cent of normal size;
1 cm = 0.7km on the ground

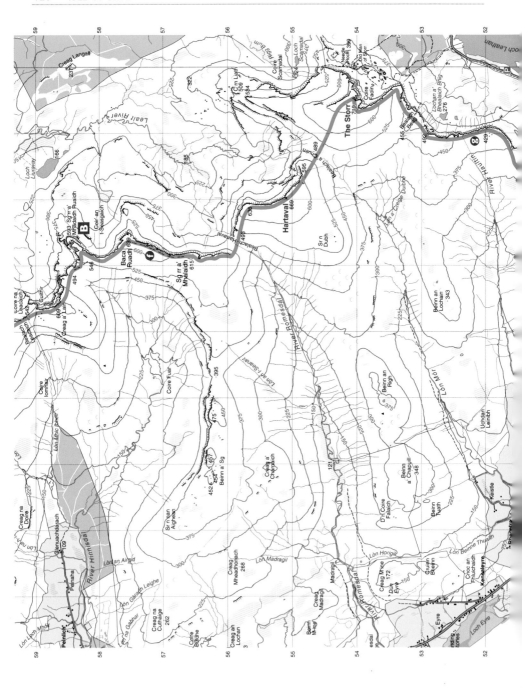

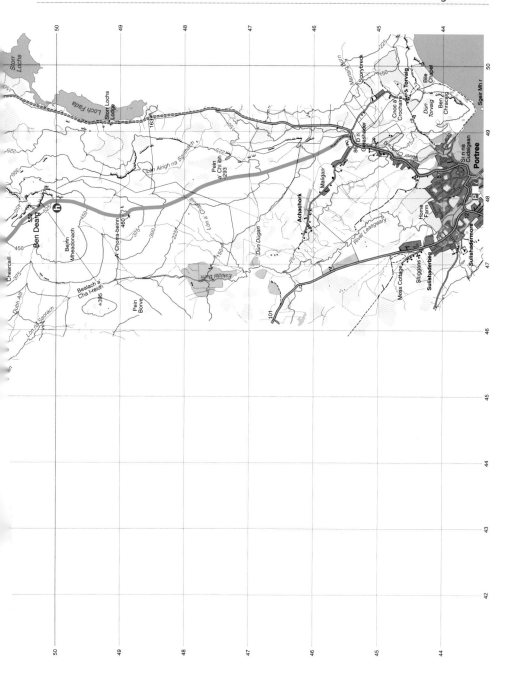

Map reproduced at 70 per cent of normal size;
1 cm = 0.7km on the ground

The Trotternish Ridge is built of sheets of basalt lava. Rather than flat like the lava that makes up MacLeod's Tables to the west the rock here slopes gently, creating a long escarpment with the dip slope to the west and the steeper scarp slope to the east. Due to the weight of the basalt sheets pressing down on the weaker sedimentary rocks below the latter subsided causing a series of enormous landslides, by far the biggest in Britain, that resulted in the shattered, dramatic scenery on the east side of the ridge. In profile the ridge has a distinctive stepped appearance, the eastern slopes being made up of a series of terraces. This is known as a 'trap' landscape. The steps are due to the separate layers of basalt lavas eroding at different rates.

girt knoll of Cleat to its left, and then on along the undulating ridge to the Storr, which looks a long way away.

d   A path leads up the first part of Biode Buidhe but fades away before the summit is reached. Looking back you can see the Quiraing in profile below Meall Suiramach. A steep descent from Biode Buidhe leads down to the Bealach nan Coisichean. A slight rise, Druim na Coille, separates this from the Bealach Uige, from where you could descend west to Uig. This is the shortest way off the ridge to a settlement. Beyond the bealach climb steadily up Beinn Edra.

A   Beinn Edra 455 627

At 2,004ft (611m) Beinn Edra is the most northerly 2,000ft- (600m-) summit on Skye and also the highest peak on the central part of the ridge. As such it's a good viewpoint for the whole ridge. To the north the Quiraing is visible while to the south the Storr doesn't look quite so distant now. And east and west the sea rolls away to islands and hills.

e   A short descent leads from Beinn Edra to the Bealach a'Mhoramhain. Next comes a short rise then another brief downhill to the Bealach Amadal from where a narrower section of ridge leads up to Groba nan Each. The rapid succession of ups and downs continues with a descent to the Bealach Chaiplin, an ascent of Flasvein, a drop to the Bealach na Leacaich and a climb to Creag a'Lain. Beyond Creag a'Lain the ridge turns to the east and runs out to Sgurr a'Mhadaidh Ruaidh.

B   Sgurr a'Mhadaidh Ruaidh 474 584

Sgurr a'Mhadaidh Ruaidh (the Peak of the Red Fox) is an unusual peak for the Trotternish Ridge. Most of the summits are high points on the south to north running escarpment. Sgurr a'Mhadaidh Ruaidh however is a tiny summit at the end of a short ridge running out to the east. There are cliffs on three sides. Unsurprisingly the views are excellent. Immediately below lies Loch Cuithir with beyond it flat moorland stretching out to the sea. The main ridge stretches out to north and south. A rough road leads to Loch Cuithir, dating from the time when diatomite was mined here, giving good access to this section of the ridge.

f   From Sgurr a'Mhadaidh Ruaidh walk round the rim of Coir'an t-Seasgaich to the little summit of Baca Ruadh. The descent to the Bealach Hartaval is quite rocky, unusual for this walk, but then the normal grassy slopes return for the ascent of Hartaval, at 2,191ft (668m) the second highest summit on the ridge. The highest peak, the Storr, lies not far away across Bealach a'Chuirn. The descent to the bealach is quite steep. From the bealach don't follow the line of crags, which here turn north-east onto a spur leading to Carn Liath, but climb south-east over broad slopes to the Storr. The view from this summit is superb. For details see Walk 9.

g A long descent beside the cliffs to the Bealach Mor follows, interrupted by a slight rise just beyond the Bealach Beag. From the Bealach Mor the cliffs running below the summit of Ben Dearg, the last peak on the ridge, look quite forbidding. To turn these head west until you can see a way up the steep slopes above.

h Ben Dearg marks the end of the cliffs and there just remains a boggy descent down to Portree. Go over the little bumps of A'Chorra-bheinn and Pent a'Chleibh and down to the A855 near the bridge over the River Chracaig. It's now 1½ miles (2.5km) down the road to the centre of Portree.

Cleat and Bioda Buidhe from the slopes of Meall na Suiramach with Beinn Edra in the distance

MARSCO

START/FINISH:
Sligachan. There are places to park just before the A850 road crosses the bridge over the River Sligachan. There are good bus connections from Portree, Broadford and Kyle of Lochalsh with Citylink, Highland Country and Skye-Ways. There are even direct buses from Glasgow.

DISTANCE:
8 miles (13km)

APPROXIMATE TIME:
4–6 hours

HIGHEST POINT:
2,414ft (736m)

MAP:
Harveys Superwalker Skye: The Cuillin

REFRESHMENTS:
The Sligachan Hotel.

ADVICE:
This is a straightforward ascent with a path much of the way. There are some steep slopes but no crags and very little scree to deal with. Navigation high up could be difficult in mist.

Marsco is perhaps the finest of the Red Hills. It stands in a commanding and somewhat isolated position above Glen Sligachan, separated from other hills by low saddles. From Sligachan Marsco looks particularly impressive, appearing as a shapely if bulky pyramid with a kink in one side that is the cliff of Fiaclan Dearg. This walk climbs to a bealach from where Marsco can be ascended and has excellent views throughout.

a The walk starts at Sligachan and follows the path down the glen as in Walk 14 as far as the Allt na Measarroch. Just before the ford there is a junction where a path heads up beside the burn. Take this path up into long narrow Coire Dubh Measarroch and on to Mam a'Phobuill at its head. The path is rough and boggy and very indistinct in places. If you lose it simply follow the burn upwards.

Marsco and the River Sligachan

Marsco and the River Sligachan

A   Mam a'Phobuill 513 260

Mam a'Phobuill is a 935ft (285m) pass between Coire Dubh Measarroch and Coire nam Bruadaran. It covers quite an extensive area and is very boggy. The name means 'Pass of the People', possibly because it was an easy route between the heads of Loch Sligachan and Loch Ainort. According to some stories Prince Charles Edward Stuart crossed the pass en route from Glen Sligachan to Loch Ainort when in hiding after the failure of the '45 uprising.

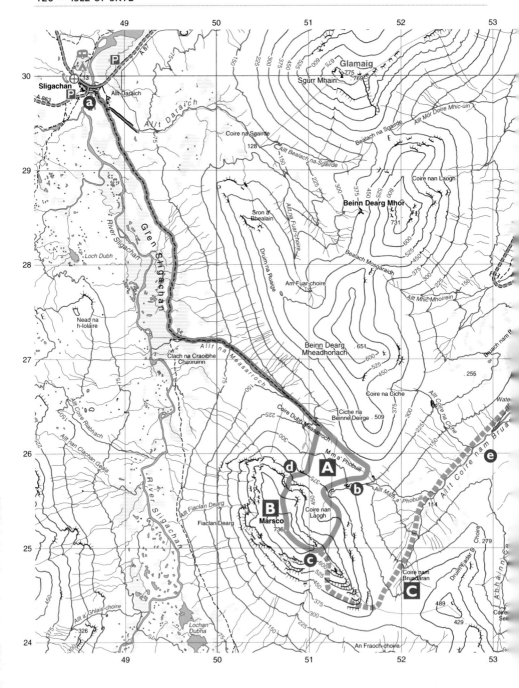

The word 'mam' is sometimes used for a pass rather than 'bealach'. It means breast and is used for a pass presumably because a pass is like the dip between two breasts.

There are superb views from the eastern end of the pass to Belig, Garbh-bheinn and Bla Bheinn. Marsco towers over the pass to the south-west, looking intimidating rather than attractive.

b A corrie curves into the slopes of Marsco above Mam a'Phobuill, a classic little corrie scooped out of the hillside. This is Coire nan Laogh (the Corrie of the Calves). The way to the summit is along the edges of this corrie. The ascent can be done either way round but I'd suggest ascending the eastern side first, as this isn't as steep as the western edge.

To reach the corrie edge you have to cross Allt Mam a'Phobuill, which flows out of the corrie in a long stream down a rock groove and then drops into a deep gorge in a waterfall you can hear roaring from the summit when the weather is calm.

Marsco

Once across the burn follow a series of old fence posts up the side of the corrie. The climb is steep in places but not difficult.

c   The ascent brings you out onto the south-east ridge of Marsco at a small dip. Follow the fairly narrow but not exposed ridge up to the small neat summit, where there is a little cairn.

B   Marsco 507 252
The tiny summit cairn is perched on a very narrow ridge. It appears to lie just beyond the highest point, where there is

barely room for a cairn. The summit ridge is an amazing viewpoint. To the south-east Bla Bheinn rises slightly behind Garbh-bheinn, which for once is not totally overshadowed by its bigger neighbour. Where Bla Bheinn is a bulky fissured wall, a solid hulk of a hill, Garbh-bheinn is more graceful, delicate even, with a short narrow summit ridge between two flowing ridges that almost encircle the deep, dark corrie below the top. Below these two hills lie the dark waters of Loch na Creithach in Srath na Creithach with the grass, beach and sea of Camasunary beyond it, all seen over the pale orange-pink screes of the little whaleback of Ruadh-stac. To the right of Camasunary rises dark and bulky Sgurr na Stri. Then comes the most exciting vista, the long black serrated line of the Cuillin, the whole ridge in view curving round the deep bowl of Harta Corrie. It's a magnificent wild sight that holds the eye as, the initial shock past, you start to take in the complexities of the scene and identify individual peaks and features. When you finally turn away, look north where Beinn Dearg Mhor appears as a graceful slim pyramid with bulky Glamaig rising behind it. To the right of these hills lies Loch Ainort and then Scalpay and other islands in the Inner Sound.

On the west face of Marsco, overlooking Glen Sligachan, is a rugged rock feature called Fiaclan Dearg (the Red Tooth). The only rock climbs in the Red Hills are found on the two buttresses of Fiaclan Dearg. The first route here was put up by Noel Odell in 1943. Odell is famous for his role in the Everest Expedition of 1924 when he was the last person to see Mallory and Irvine high on the mountain before they disappeared. The route is called Odell's Route and is graded Difficult.

Marsco is a Norse word meaning Seagull Mountain, presumably because gulls were seen here. It's classified as a Graham in Scottish mountain lists, that is a summit between 2,000 and 2,500ft (610–762m) high.

d From the summit head north then north-east down the spur that forms the northern side of Coire nan Laogh. The going is quite rough and steep in the middle of the descent. Eventually a steep tongue of grass leads down to the mouth of the corrie from where easier slopes lead back to Mam a'Phobuill and the path back down Allt na Measarroch to Glen Sligachan.

e There is a shorter but less scenic way up Marsco. This starts at the head of Loch Ainort where the road crosses the

The southern Cuillin from the summit of Marsco

Allt Coire nam Bruadaran by a fine and much photographed waterfall. Follow the burn up over very boggy ground into Coire nam Bruadaran. As you approach the bealach at the head of the corrie angle right onto the south-east ridge of Marsco and follow it to the summit. Descent can be by either of the sides of Coire nan Laogh to Mam a'Phobuill from where you can descend back to the Allt Coire nam Bruadaran.

C   Coire nam Bruadaran 520 246

Coire nam Bruadaran has the wonderful meaning of Corrie of Dreams. Why it has this evocative name is unknown, no legends remaining. This of course allows for unrestrained speculation. In his book The Heart of Skye Jim Crumley devotes a whole chapter to Coire nam Bruadaran in which he conjures up a magical story as to how the corrie, along with Coire nam Laogh, got its name.

GLAMAIG AND THE BEINN DEARGS

The Western Red Hills are big bulky scree-covered hills lying between Lochs Ainort and Sligachan. The climb to their summits is steep but leads to superb ridge walking with excellent views.

a   The walk starts at Sligachan. Go through the stile in the fence to the east of the old bridge over the River Sligachan and walk a very short distance along the path down the glen to where a path branches off along the right (true left) bank of the Allt Daraich.

A   Allt Daraich Gorge 487 297
In its lower reaches the Allt Daraich runs down a deep wooded gorge. On the southern slopes there is a fine stand of aspens whilst to the north Allt Daraich house (where there is bunkhouse accommodation) sits on a knoll surrounded by Scots pine and other trees. There are attractive waterfalls and deep pools in the gorge. Above the gorge the burn is a pleasant mountain stream running through boggy moorland.

b   The path peters out above the gorge. The burn can then be followed into the mouth of Coire na Sgairde where you turn south and head up Sron a'Bhealain at the end of Druim na Ruaige. It is slightly shorter but far less interesting and wetter underfoot to head straight across the moor from the end of the gorge to the foot of Sron a'Bhealain.

START/FINISH:
Sligachan. There are places to park just before the A850 road crosses the bridge over the River Sligachan. There are good bus connections from Portree, Broadford and Kyle of Lochalsh with Citylink, Highland Country and Skye-Ways. There are even direct buses from Glasgow.

DISTANCE:
7 miles (11km)

APPROXIMATE TIME:
5–7 hours

HIGHEST POINT:
2,542ft (775m) Glamaig

MAP:
Harveys Superwalker Skye: The Cuillin

REFRESHMENTS:
The Sligachan Hotel.

ADVICE:
The round of the Western Red Hills isn't difficult but it is arduous as much of the terrain is steep. Navigation can be difficult in mist.

Glamaig (left), Beinn Dearg Mhor and Beinn Dearg Mheadhonach from Marsco

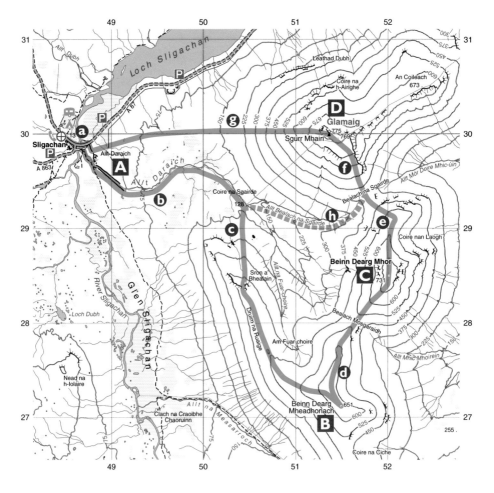

c Climb the steep, grassy slopes of Sron a'Bhealain to long level Druim na Ruaige, which leads to the west ridge of Beinn Dearg Mheadhonach. A rough path leads up the steep scree to the summit ridge. There are cairns at each end. That at the far (south-east) end is the highest.

B Beinn Dearg Mheadhonach 515 271
Beinn Dearg Mheadhonach means Middle Red Hill. This isn't a demeaning reference to its height but rather means that it lies in the centre or heart of the hills and Beinn Dearg Mheadhonach does indeed lie in the centre of the Western Red Hills, which line the east side of Glen Sligachan from Ruadh Stac to Glamaig.

Beinn Dearg Mheadhonach (left), Glamaig and Beinn Dearg Mhor from Marsco

Beinn Dearg Mheadhonach's narrow summit ridge is over 800ft (250m) long giving it a cut-off appearance in contrast to the pointed summit of Beinn Dearg Mhor and the rounded dome of Glamaig. The high point is 2,135ft (651m) above sea level. It's a great viewpoint for Loch Ainort as it stands directly above the head of the loch. Further east Beinn na Caillich and the other hills of the Coire Gorm horseshoe (see Walk 17) are in view. Beyond them can be seen the bridge to the mainland. To the north Beinn Dearg Mhor appears as a pale thin steep pyramid with bulky Glamaig behind it. Across Glen Sligachan Sgurr nan Gillean looks very impressive with the rest of the Cuillin curving away to the south. The great wedge of the Inaccessible Pinnacle stands out prominently on Sgurr Dearg (see Walk 29) and Sgurr Alasdair is visible as the highest summit near the far end of the Cuillin.

d Walk back along the ridge from the summit then descend the north ridge of Beinn Dearg Mheadhonach to the Bealach Mosgaraidh at 1,673ft (510m) and continue up the ridge on the far side to Beinn Dearg Mhor. This is a fine ridge walk with excellent views. The walking is on scree and rock but although the terrain is quite steep, especially on the ascent of Beinn Dearg Mhor, it is not anywhere difficult. The large boulders give better walking than the scree.

C Beinn Dearg Mhor 520 284
Beinn Dearg Mhor has quite a small pointed summit, unusual in the Red Hills. The summit cairn is tall and well made rather than the usual pile of stones. The view is excellent, though unsurprisingly very similar to that from Beinn Dearg Mheadhonach, especially down Loch Ainort to the island of Scalpay and south to Garbh-bheinn and Bla Bheinn. You can

Glamaig, Beinn Dearg Mhor and Beinn Dearg Mheadhonach

see the A850 winding round the hillside practically below your feet, the speeding vehicles looking like tiny toys. The one unique view is ahead to Glamaig, seen in full from here as a long gently curving ridge with the main big dome of a summit at one end and a small rise to a minor top at the other.

Beinn Dearg Mhor is the Big Red Hill, after the pink granite screes on its flanks. Together with Beinn Dearg Mheadhonach it forms a pale centrepiece between the darker grey slopes of Marsco and Glamaig.

At 2,398ft (731m) and with a big drop between it and Glamaig Beinn Dearg Mhor is classified as a Graham, that is a Scottish peak between 2,000 and 2,500ft (610–762m).

e A long steep descent leads from the summit of Beinn Dearg Mhor down slopes of rock and scree for over 1,000ft (300m) to the Bealach na Sgairde (Scree Pass) at 1,361ft (415m). Care needs to be taken to leave the ridge lower down where it curves to the north-east and descend west of north to the bealach. This is especially so in mist.

f From the bealach climb straight up the steep slopes of Glamaig. The rock rib to the right – up which you can scramble if you wish – is made from basalt that was pushed up by the granites that form the bulk of the mountain. The ascent reaches the summit ridge a little east of the trig point.

D Glamaig 513 300
Like many mountains that are in fact long ridges with more than one summit there is an overall name plus names for the

individual peaks. Glamaig is the name for the whole hill, the highest summit being called Sgurr Mhairi, which means Mary's Peak. The smaller top at the north-east end of the summit ridge is An Coileach, meaning Little Cock, as in grouse cock. The meaning of Glamaig itself seems a little obscure as it is given as Gorge Mountain by Peter Drummond in Scottish Hill and Mountain Names but in other places such as the SMC Hillwalkers' Guide to The Corbetts as Greedy Woman. The first would seem to make more sense as the Allt Daraich gorge lies on its lower slopes.

At 2,542ft (775m) Glamaig is the only one of the Red Hills to reach 2,500ft (762m), hence its designation in mountain lists as a Corbett, that is a peak in the Highlands between 2,500 and 3,000ft (762–915m).

Whatever the derivation of its name Glamaig, because of its height and its situation on the coast and to the north of the other mountains, is a wonderful viewpoint with huge panoramic vistas spread out on every side. Unsurprisingly Sgurr nan Gillean across Glen Sligachan is particularly impressive. The rest of the Cuillin looks good too. To the north Ben Tianavaig (see Walk 10) can be seen as a tilted plateau, mirroring the profile of the Storr, which can be seen beyond it. Way beyond Trotternish and stretching down to the south lie the Outer Isles. Westwards Raasay and Scalpay and the other islands in the Inner Sound can be seen with the mainland hills of Torridon and Applecross behind them. To the

Glamaig from Beinn Dearg Mhor

south Bla Bheinn dominates the view. And down to the east, very close it seems though a long way below, lies Sligachan.

To mountain runners Sligachan really is very close, astonishingly close in fact. Way back in 1899 a Ghurka called Havildar Harkabir Thapa ran to the summit and back in an amazing 55 minutes – 37 minutes up and 18 minutes down – from the Sligachan Hotel. He did it in bare feet too. His record lasted for 90 years, being finally broken in 1989 in the second annual Glamaig hill race, which was set up in part to commemorate Harkabir Thapa's feat. The current record is an almost unbelievable 46 minutes. Of course today's runners wear shoes.

Although granite makes up most of Glamaig the summit is in fact capped with basalt, pushed up by the granite during the volcanic action that created the Red Hills.

g The descent from Glamaig is very simple, at least as far as route finding goes. Just aim for Sligachan. Much of the descent is on steep scree. There are some grassy rakes that can be followed, especially lower down, though these can be slippery when wet. As you descend just think of running down in 18 minutes.

h If you don't fancy the knee-hammering direct descent return to the Bealach na Sgairde and descend into Coire na Sgairde. Follow the Allt Bealach na Sgairde down to the Allt Daraich, which can be followed in turn to join the outward route.

Glamaig

GARBH-BHEINN AND BELIG

Garbh-bheinn is a fine rocky peak rising above the head of Loch Ainort. Its ascent involves a little easy scrambling. It can easily be linked to Belig to make an excellent horseshoe walk with good views throughout.

A Eas a'Bhradain 533 265

Just up the road from the lay-by the Allt Coire nam Bruadaran (the Burn of the Corrie of Dreams – see Walk 19) comes crashing down in a big impressive waterfall that must be one of the most photographed in Scotland. This is the Eas a'Bhradain (Robber's Fall according to Hamish Brown in Climbing the Corbetts but Salmon Fall according to Louis Stott in The Waterfalls of Scotland).

a Start the walk by heading across the boggy heather moorland between the Allt Coire nam Bruadaran and the Abhainn Ceann Loch Ainort (River of the Head of Loch Ainort) towards Druim Eadar Da Choire (the Ridge between the Corries). This stony ridge separates Coire nam Bruadaran, which belongs to Marsco, and Coire na Seilg, nestling below the summit of Garbh-bheinn. There are traces of a path in the heather but it's not worth trying to link these. To the right Marsco and the two Beinn Dearg hills rise steeply while ahead Garbh-bheinn looks quite daunting.

b Ascend Druim Eadar Da Choire to its little 1,603ft-(489m-) summit and a grand view of the southern end of the

START/FINISH:
Large lay-by on the A850 at the head of Loch Ainort (536 265). Citylink, Highland Country and Skye-Ways run buses between Broadford and Portree and may put down passengers at this point if requested.

DISTANCE:
5 miles (8km)

APPROXIMATE TIME:
4–6 hours

HIGHEST POINT:
2,644ft (806m) Garbh-bheinn

MAP:
Harveys Superwalker Skye: The Cuillin

REFRESHMENTS:
To the north the Sligachan Hotel, to the south Broadford.

ADVICE:
There are steep rocky slopes high up on Garbh-bheinn where hands may be required in places. These sections are very short. Much of the walking is on steep rough terrain however. Lower down the ground can be very wet.

Garbh-bheinn (left), Clach Glas and Bla Bheinn

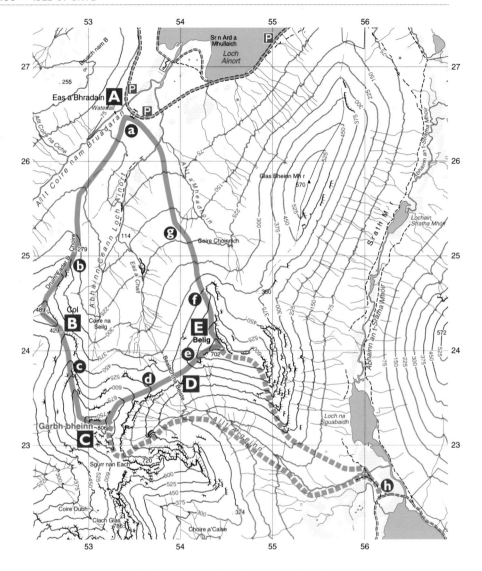

Cuillin. Descend briefly along a line of rusty old fence posts to a small but significant unnamed col.

B Col 527 242

On this col the granite of the Red Hills meets the gabbro of the Cuillin and the change can be seen clearly in the colour of the rock here, which changes abruptly from pale to dark. Ahead the rough rock strewn slopes of Garbh-bheinn show the difference to the hills the type of rock makes, especially when

Belig

you look back to the rounded, smoother slopes of Marsco and the Beinn Deargs. The change in the rock type can also be seen from the start of the walk and from Belig (and from other viewpoints further away) with Druim Eadar Da Choire a pale hump just below the dark grey of the north ridge of Garbh-bheinn.

c The rusting fence posts continue up the north ridge of Garbh-bheinn from the col. A path winds up the scree and rock close to them. Near the summit where the ridge turns to the left it becomes very narrow and the boulders grow larger so that some scrambling is required. The easiest ground lies to the right (south) here.

C Garbh-bheinn 531 232
The summit of Garbh-bheinn is a tiny perch surmounted by a small cairn. The name means Rough Hill and it is certainly

appropriate for up here all is rock and stone. Bla Bheinn dominates the view, a massive tangle of chaotic rock rearing up immediately to the south. It is very close but not reachable from here by the walker as the great rock tower of Clach Glas, known as the 'Matterhorn of Skye', blocks the way. The easiest way up this, one of the most difficult summits on Skye, is graded Moderate – moderate to rock climbers, that is. And even if you manage to negotiate Clach Glas the way up Bla Bheinn is then even harder and is graded Difficult though there is an easier scramble that avoids the initial difficulties (see Noel Williams' Skye Scrambles for details).

Turning away from the overpowering sight of Bla Bheinn you can look back to the Western Red Hills and out over Loch Ainort to the Inner Sound and its islands with the mainland hills on the horizon. To the east across Loch Slapin the hills of the Coire Gorm Horseshoe (see Walk 17) form a distinct, compact group of pale rounded, steep-sided summits. The Cuillin, which attract the attention for much of the ascent, lie to the west.

d   Leave the summit by the north-east ridge. This is steep and loose at the top, requiring care but soon becomes easier. The ridge leads to a fairly wide pass, the Bealach na Beiste, at 1,493ft (455m).

D   Bealach na Beiste 539 237
An entertaining legend attaches to the Bealach na Beiste, which means the Pass of the Beast. It is said that Mackinnon of Strath killed a 'beast' on this pass. It is also said that this creature may have been a water horse that had been causing trouble down at Loch na Sguabaidh, which lies in Srath Mor

to the east of Garbh-bheinn and which can be seen from the summit. This water horse had been running off with any pretty girls who came near. Plain girls were apparently safe, so much so that any girl who escaped the clutches of the water horse was then known for her beauty.

e Above the bealach steep, rough slopes lead up the south-west ridge of Belig. There are a few small crags, which are easily turned. The ridge is broad at first, with many boulders, but narrows higher up where a ruined dry stone wall leads to the summit. There is a rough path to the left (north) of the wall. In the wet the top of the mountain can be slippery as the rocks are basalt here not the gabbro that is found lower down.

E   Belig 544 240

Belig is the true northern end of the Cuillin Outliers, the gabbro ridge running from Bla Bheinn over Clach Glas and Garbh-bheinn. A tiny cairn sits on the narrow summit ridge. There is a good view south over the deep bowl of the Allt Aigeinn to the north face of Sgurr nan Each, a vast mass of crosshatched cliffs, gullies and stone chutes. Behind Sgurr nan Each, which lies on a spur between Garbh-bheinn and Clach Glas, rises the much higher summit of Bla Bheinn. Looking back Garbh-bheinn appears as a pyramid rising steeply above the Bealach na Beiste. To the north-east rises the long ridge of Glas Bheinn Mhor, an isolated Red Hills summit that can be linked with Belig by descending just south of east from the summit a little way then turning more steeply northwards and dropping down to the col between the two hills. To the north and east Loch Ainort can be seen along with Glamaig, the Beinn Deargs and Marsco. Further east lie the Cuillin.

Belig is 2,303ft (702m) high and is classified as a Graham, a summit between 2,000 and 2,500ft (610–762m). The meaning of the name, which is Norse, is unknown.

f   The north ridge of Belig is a mix of grass and stone with crags on the eastern side. It's quite narrow but the walk down it is without difficulties until a steep nose of broken crags is reached at 543 246. With care a way can be found through the crags. The easiest ground is on the crest or just slightly to the left (west).

g   Once below the nose head across the increasingly boggy moorland down the broad spur between the Allt a'Mheadhoin and the Abhainn Ceann Loch Ainort and back to the start.

THE CUILLIN OUTLIERS
Garbh-bheinn and Belig are part of the Cuillin Outliers, a small group of gabbro peaks cut off from the main Cuillin by Srath na Creitheach. Bla Bheinn (see Walk 22) is the highest of this group. Like the main Cuillin these are impressive rock peaks with narrow ridges, huge cliffs, rock pinnacles and other features. All can be reached by walking routes except for Clach Glas, which requires rock-climbing skills.

h An alternative and equally excellent route up Belig and Garbh-bheinn starts at the head of Loch Slapin (562 224). There is a magnificent view of the Cuillin Outliers from Bla Bheinn to Belig here. The route crosses boggy ground to ford the Allt Aigeine and then ascend the south-east ridge of Belig. The initial climb is on steep grass with occasional small crags. The easiest ground is to the right (east). There is a view east to three almost matching whaleback shaped hills – Beinn na Cro, Beinn Dearg Mhor and Beinn Dearg Bheag. Higher up the ground becomes steeper and more rocky and the ridge narrows. Here the easiest ground is on the left (west). There are places where hands will probably be needed but the scrambling is easy.

From the summit reverse the route between Belig and Garbh-bheinn described above, descending to the Bealach na Beiste then climbing the north-east ridge of Garbh-bheinn. Descend the south-east ridge next. This is steep and loose at the top but soon becomes easier though it remains rough and rocky with much scree. From the bealach you can climb south a short way to view the huge cliffs of Clach Glas. The descent is from the bealach into the glen of the Allt Aigeinn. There are scree and boulders at first, then grass and bog. The Allt Aigeinn is a delightful burn with a series of waterfalls, one a serpentine twist of water in a long rock chute, another a double fall in a tree-lined gorge. There are beautiful pools too, with smooth curved rock walls. The stream can be followed to the outward route.

Belig

BLA BHEINN

Bla Bheinn is one of the finest mountains in the Highlands, a magnificent huge wedge of rock. Most of the mountain is accessible only to climbers but the south ridge is a superb scenic walker's route, one of the best on Skye. It's a satisfyingly direct ascent, straight from beautiful Camasunary Bay to the summit with wonderful views of the main Cuillin ridge throughout. Bla Bheinn is shaped like a graceful arrowhead (just look at the contours on the map) and this route runs from the tip right up the centre of this arrowhead.

a The walk begins some 400 yards (365m) past the Kilmarie junction on the Broadford-Elgol road. A stile and gate gives access to a track. It's an unpromising start, following this ugly bulldozed 4WDvehicle track (see Walk 15) that runs over the shallow pass of Am Mam (the Breast) to Camasunary. The view is inspiring though with the Cuillin summits rising beyond Am Mam. Bla Bheinn however is hidden by the moorland slopes of Slat Bheinn.

b A massive cairn marks the top of Am Mam. Just over the top the south ridge of Bla Bheinn is seen for the first time. The long, long rocky ridge can look daunting from here but the ascent is not as hard or as lengthy as it appears. Descend the track for around ½ mile (800m) as it curves towards the south ridge to a junction just before it doglegs sharply to the left.

START/FINISH:
Kilmarie (545 172) on the Broadford to Elgol road. There is room to park by the road here. There is a post bus to Elgol that may drop you off here if requested.

DISTANCE:
7½ miles (12km)

APPROXIMATE TIME:
5–8 hours

HIGHEST POINT:
3,044ft (928m)

MAP:
Harveys Superwalker Skye: The Cuillin

REFRESHMENTS:
Cafes in Elgol or Broadford.

ADVICE:
The terrain for most of this walk is rough and rocky. There is a very short scramble near the end. Navigation can be difficult in mist.

Garbhbheinn (left) and Bla Bheinn

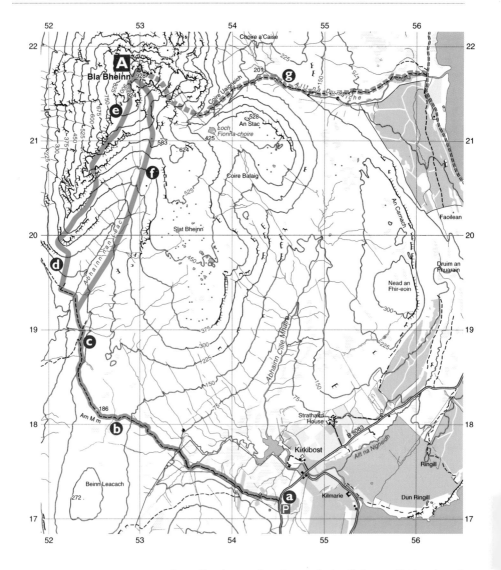

c A small cairn marks where a footpath leaves the track and heads north to the Abhainn nan Leac, a fine stream with some attractive small waterfalls. A couple of hundred yards (200m) beyond the burn look for another path junction at the foot of the south ridge. Turn right here and start the ascent.

d The ascent is simple now. Just keep on up the ridge. Initially the ridge is grassy but it soon becomes rocky with small outcrops on the ridge and crags on either side. The path winds in and out round small crags and the heads of deep gullies. Those who wish can scramble up the rocks.

e   The south ridge ends at the south top (3,030ft/924m), a small stony summit with a fine view. The main summit is only 200 yards (180m) to the north-east but the hardest part of the walk lies in between the two tops. This is the descent from the south top. There are two ways to tackles this. The easiest is by a steep dirt gully that finishes just below the dip between the two tops. Slightly harder is the descent of the rock steps directly to the col. These are both scrambles, albeit easy ones. The rock steps are more exposed than the gully. From the dip the final climb to the summit is simple.

A   Bla Bheinn 530 217

The glory of Bla Bheinn lies in the mountain itself rather than the view from the summit. That said, there is a stupendous view, especially east across deep Srath na Creithach to the main Cuillin ridge, all of which is in view.

At 3,044ft (928m) Bla Bheinn is the only summit on Skye outside the main Cuillin ridge that reaches 3,000ft (915m). That means it is the only summit on Skye that is the equal of the Cuillin, the only one from which you can view the Cuillin from the same height. From all other viewpoints the Cuillin look bigger, higher, more mountainous. Not from Bla Bheinn. Here you feel you are on a mountain just as rugged, just as high, just as grand.

Like the Cuillin Bla Bheinn is built of gabbro and its steep flanks harbour a mass of rock climbs of all standards. To the north of the summit the north-east face descends very steeply

Garb-bheinn (left) and Bla Bheinn

Garb-bheinn (left), Clach Glas and Bla Bheinn from Marsco

to the dip, known as the Putting Green, below Clach Glas. The direct descent of the face is a rock climb though there are scrambles to either side that bypass the hardest rocks. Even if you can reach the bealach Clach Glas then bars the way and any way of that rock tower involves rock climbing. The west face is a mass of big cliffs and slabs riven by scree gullies up which an experienced scrambler might find a way. Only the southern part of the east face offers any easy way for walkers other than the south face.

Tearing your eyes away from the Cuillin you can look north to Garbh-bheinn, which looks small and delicate, fragile almost, from here. To its right lie the rounded summits of the Red Hills, pleasant hills but from up here on this rocky eyrie they are just hills, not mountains. To the east the Coire Gorm Horseshoe looks similarly diminished. One reason for climbing those lesser hills is for the view of Bla Bheinn, something that is clearly understood on the summit of Bla Bheinn. Back down the south ridge you can look over Camasunary to the sea and the spiky islands of Rum and Eigg.

Bla Bheinn is the favourite of many who walk and climb on Skye going right back to Sheriff Alexander Nicolson who said it was the finest on Skye. He was a native of the island and one of the early mountaineers. In 1872 he made the first ascent of the highest peak on Skye, Sgurr Alasdair, which is named after him (Alasdair being the Gaelic form of Alexander). The first recorded climb of Bla Bheinn was much earlier however, in 1857, and achieved by a very unlikely pair of climbers, the poet Algernon Swinburne and John Nicol, a Professor of English. Both, in the words of Ian Mitchell

(Scotland's Mountains Before The Mountaineers), were 'inveterate drunkards'. At the time they believed Bla Bheinn was the highest mountain on Skye, a view, says Mitchell, they shared with no one else. This ascent was the only contribution either of them made to the history of mountaineering on Skye.

Bla Bheinn is a mix of Norse (Bla) and Gaelic (Bheinn). It means Blue Mountain, from the bluish tinge it has when seen from a distance (a property shared with many mountains). The name is sometimes anglicised to Blaven.

f   To descend the mountain back to the start, return across the dip to the south summit. The route can then be varied by either descending south to the Abhainn nan Leac and following this down to the path or descending south-east along the edge of Coire Uaigneich and then descending more slowly across the boggy, lochan-dotted moorland of Slat Bheinn to the Am Mam track.

g   An alternative and more popular ascent route, shorter than the south ridge and avoiding the scramble below the south top but nowhere near as scenic or interesting, starts on the Broadford-Elgol road by the bridge over the Allt Dunaiche (561 217). A path follows the Allt Dunaiche past a wooded gorge and some waterfalls. After almost a mile (1.5km) the path crosses the stream and starts to climb into Coire Uaigneich. The very steep cliffs of the east face of Bla Bheinn loom over you at this point. Once in the corrie turn right and climb the steep hillside to the summit, first over grass and then over rock and scree. There is a cairned path the whole way plus opportunities for scrambling.

Bla Bheinn from Marsco

SGURR BEAG AND HARTA AND LOTA CORRIES

START/FINISH:
Sligachan. There are places to park just before the A850 road crosses the bridge over the River Sligachan. There are good bus connections from Portree, Broadford and Kyle of Lochalsh with Citylink, Highland Country and Skye-Ways. There are even direct buses from Glasgow.

DISTANCE:
11 miles (18km) via Coire Riabhach 12 miles (20km) via Bealach nan Lice

APPROXIMATE TIME:
5–7 hours

HIGHEST POINT:
2,509ft (765m) Sgurr Beag via Coire Riabhach, 2,935ft (895m) via Bealach nan Lice.

MAP:
Harveys Superwalker Skye: The Cuillin

REFRESHMENTS:
The Sligachan Hotel.

ADVICE:
This is a long walk into two remote corries. As far as Harta Corrie it is an easy if boggy walk, mostly on a path and on flat or gently sloping terrain. From Harta Corrie onwards the terrain is much steeper and rougher and good route-finding skills are required.

The northern end of the Cuillin curls tightly round remote Harta and Lota Corries, hiding them from view. These are dramatic corries, walled in by rock peaks and ridges. From Lota Corrie you can climb Sgurr Beag, a minor top on the south ridge of Sgurr nan Gillean, which is a superb viewpoint for the two corries and for the northern Cuillin. Alternatively you can climb to the Bealach nan Lice, set in a wonderful situation below the Bhasteir Tooth, and then descend Fionn Choire.

a   The walk starts at Sligachan (see Walk 14). From the gate in the fence near the old bridge take the path down Glen

Sligachan past the boulder of Clach na Craoibhe Chaoruinn and on under the slopes of Marsco (see Walk 19).

b After 3½ miles (5.5km) the River Sligachan makes a sharp turn to the right. The two Lochan Dubhe can be seen just beyond the turn. The watershed between Loch Sligachan and Loch Scavaig lies between these two lochans while to their right is the mouth of Harta Corrie, dominated here by the truncated south ridge of Sgurr nan Gillean, which ends in the spire of Sgurr na h-Uamha. Once you are level with the bend in the river look out for a wide grassy break in the heather and bog running down to the right. Leave the main path and walk down this to pick up a rough, wet path where the break ends. This path leads down to the River Sligachan and then follows the river upstream into Harta Corrie.

Harta Corrie and the northern Cuillin

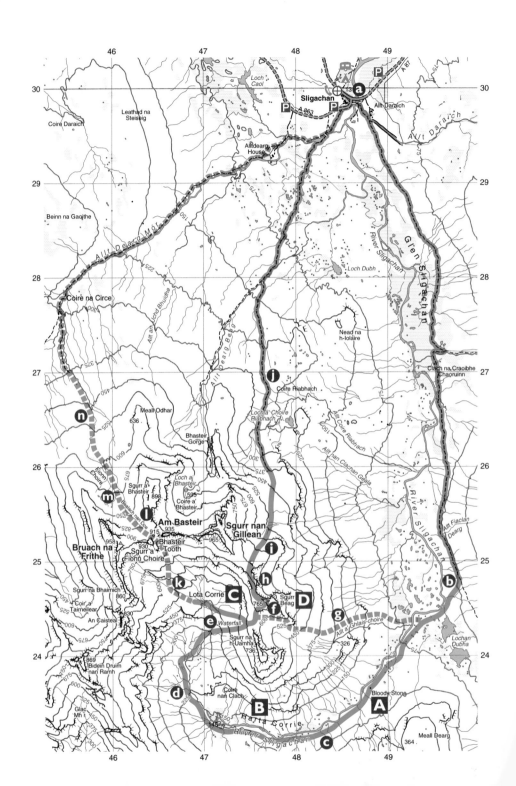

A The Bloody Stone 488 237

In the mouth of the corrie a massive boulder capped with a miniature wood of rowans and other shrubs sits on the southern slopes just above the river. This is the Bloody Stone, so called because of yet another fight between the MacLeods and the MacDonalds. After the battle, depending on which account of the story you read, either the bodies of the slaughtered MacLeods were piled round the stone by the victorious MacDonalds or the victorious MacLeods divided up their spoils round the stone.

The boulder overhangs at the east end and would provide good shelter on a wet day.

c   The path continues, wetly, a short way beyond the Bloody Stone then disappears in the peat hags and heather. Stay with the stream, curving under the end of the massive steep-sided pyramid of Sgurr na h-Uamha and into Harta Corrie. Some walkers may prefer to finish the walk here and retrace their steps to Sligachan as the terrain ahead is much steeper and the route finding much more difficult.

B Harta Corrie 470 234

At first all that can be seen as you enter long Harta Corrie are the huge walls of Sgurr na h-Uamha on the right and the long level ridge of Druim nan Ramh (see Walk 24) on the left. However as you round the foot of Sgurr na h-Uamha the jagged rock peaks of the main Cuillin ridge slowly come into view above the vast western wall of the corrie. The dark broken pyramid of Bidein Druim nan Ramh appears first, then the squat towers of An Caisteal and Sgurr na Bhairnich and flat-topped Bruach na Frithe (see Walk 25), looking small and insignificant even though it is higher than the surrounding peaks because it is farther away. The stubby turret of Sgurr Fionn Choire is next followed by the dramatic, distinctive Basteir Tooth, a huge wedge of rock angling out from Am Basteir. Finally as you enter the heart of the corrie the spire of Sgurr nan Gillean soars up to the north.

The River Sligachan curves round beneath the jutting prow of Sgurr na h-Uamha. Once past this peak the stream runs roughly north-south instead of west-east. The slopes also start to rise noticeably, having only climbed 540ft (165m) since Sligachan. The stream drops from the upper corrie in a series of small falls and slides and is suddenly much wilder than the placid meandering river it is for much of its length.

Above the falls the angle eases off. Gently sloping upper

Sgurr na h-Uamha from Druim nan Ramh

Harta Corrie is deep in the heart of the mountains, a secluded little basin that feels strangely peaceful given the wildness of the surrounding rock walls. At the head of the corrie is an impressive wall of huge curving gabbro slabs down which the stream crashes in a long 300ft- (180m-) mix of water slides and waterfalls.

Harta Corrie is the Corrie of the Hart and this is indeed one of the few places in the Cuillin where red deer may be seen.

d Walk up the slopes beside the stream into the upper corrie. The rock slabs at the head of the corrie appear to bar further progress but there is a way to circumvent them. About a hundred yards before the falls turn right and climb about 650ft (200m) up the steep scree, rock and grass slopes to a wide shelf at about 1,650ft (500m). Follow this terrace leftwards past the top of the falls to where you can descend easily into Lota Corrie. Some writers mention cairns along this route but I found none here in 2000. Beware of going too high as higher terraces lead left onto steeper, more awkward terrain.

C   Lota Corrie 471 244

Lota Corrie is lovely, a green bowl full of rushing burns set below walls of rock. Shining threads of water slide down these walls to collect here into one stream that then thunders down into Harta Corrie. These streams are of course the headwaters of the River Sligachan. In the centre of the corrie the streams slide over gabbro slabs beside grassy slopes. On a sunny day it's a beautiful place to sit and relax, with the sound of running water all around. Above a huge unbroken rock wall curves round from the Bealach a'Bhasteir over Sgurr nan Gillean and Sgurr Beag to Sgurr na h-Uamha. Because of the closeness of the ridge the view is very foreshortened and the peaks, even Sgurr nan Gillean, look no more than bumps. Left of the Bealach a'Bhasteir the ridge is more broken and Am Basteir and the Basteir Tooth are a little more prominent. However the peak that stands out is the dark rock tower rock of Sgurr a'Fionn Choire.

The name means Lofty Corrie, very appropriate for this classic glaciated hanging valley.

e There is a choice to be made in Lota Corrie. The route onwards can be via either the Bealach nan Lice between the Bhasteir Tooth and Sgurr a'Fionn Choire (see k below) or via Sgurr Beag and Coire Riabhach. For the latter route go to the south-east corner of the corrie where steep slopes lead upwards to Bealach a'Ghlas-choire (Pass of the Grey Corrie). Retrace your steps up these slopes to the terrace that gave access from Harta Corrie. Above this point the mountainside is broken and rugged, a mix of small slabs, loose gullies and sloping terraces of grass and scree. A way can be made up this slope but it is awkward and care needs to be taken with route finding. (This is particularly so in descent). An easier alternative is to return along the terrace to the top of the ascent out of Harta Corrie and then climb the slopes above, which although loose and broken are less steep and craggy than those above Lota Corrie, until you are under the walls of Sgurr na h-Uamha. Turn left here and walk along the shelf below the cliffs to the pass.

f   From the bealach walk north up a broad ridge of grass and stones to Sgurr Beag.

D   Sgurr Beag 477 246

2,509ft- (765m-) Sgurr Beag is really just a bump on the south ridge of Sgurr nan Gillean. The name means Little Peak. The view is superb however. Sgurr nan Gillean rises to the north as a fine, almost delicate, tapering spire. Across the green depths of Lota Corrie the ridge sweeps round south from Am Basteir to Bidein Druim nan Ramh and on to Sgurr Dubh Mor. Across Glen Sligachan the Cuillin Outliers are all in view from Belig to Bla Bheinn with the Red Hills to their left. Portree can be seen too with the stepped profile of the Storr rising beyond it.

To the south rises the steep dark wedge of Sgurr na h-Uamha, the Peak of the Cave, the abrupt end of the south ridge running of Sgurr nan Gillean. The glacier that once filled Harta Corrie sliced off the ridge here to create the huge south face of Sgurr na h-Uamha.

Sgurr na h-Uamha can also be climbed from the Bealach a'Ghlas-choire but the ascent is a very different proposition, involving exposed scrambling and some Moderate grade rock climbing. You have to descend the same way too so this climb is for confident, competent scramblers only.

It would also be possible to continue on from Sgurr Beag to Sgurr nan Gillean (see Walk 28) but again note that this is a much more difficult ascent.

g   There are two options for the return to Sligachan. The easiest is to return to Bealach a'Ghlas-choire and then descend into An Glas-choire and follow the Allt a'Ghlais-choire to the River Sligachan. The descent, on stones and grass at first, then through bogs and heather, isn't steep and there are no difficulties. However to reach the main path in Glen Sligachan the river has to be forded, which could be difficult or dangerous after heavy rain. If a ford is impossible you could walk out along the left (west) bank but this would be a long and probably tedious walk over very boggy ground.

h   The shortest way back to Sligachan is to continue along the ridge from Sgurr Beag towards Sgurr nan Gillean. Halfway between the two peaks a gully descends to the right. This is where the ascent route to the south-east ridge of Sgurr nan Gillean (see Walk 28) reaches the ridge. The gully leads into a small very rocky corrie. Although there are cairns and the route is well used it can be difficult in poor visibility to locate the start of the descent. It would be better to go down An Glas-choire than risk descending in the wrong place.

i   Head north from the corrie below the vast rock walls and spires of Pinnacle Ridge on a path that descends steep, rough slopes into Coire Riabhach. The path traverses the side of the corrie well above little Loch a'Choire Riabhach.

j   The path now heads across boggy moorland to a bridge over the Allt Dearg Beag and then, just before Sligachan, another bridge, this time over the Allt Dearg Mor.

k   Returning to Lota Corrie an alternative way back to Sligachan is via the Bealach nan Lice (Pass of the Flat Stones), a route that could also include an ascent of Bruach na Frithe (see Walk 25). This is a longer, more complex route but well worth doing if there is time. To reach the Bealach nan Lice follow the left (east) branch of the stream in Lota Corrie. Where a side stream comes in from the right climb up a grassy rake beside this to where the ground levels out and the streams turns to the left. Cross a shallow bowl and go up a spur to the base of the dark cliffs of Sgurr a'Fionn Choire. Curve round the cliffs on scree and boulders to the foot of a broad stone chute that leads up to Bealach nan Lice. Just below this point a stream drops into a ravine. The ascent of the stone chute is arduous but not difficult or exposed. The easiest going at the start is on the left under the dripping, overhanging walls of Sgurr a'Fionn Choire. Higher up moving out into the centre of the chute where you can walk on larger rocks and boulders is probably easier. Throughout the ascent the huge cracked rock walls of Am Basteir and the Basteir Tooth dominate the scene, hanging menacingly above you.

l   If you want to ascend Bruach na Frithe before descending go round the north side of the stubby tower of Sgurr a'Fionn Choire from Bealach nan Lice and climb the east ridge to the summit triangulation point. This is, in Cuillin terms, an easy walk. It's also possible to scramble over Sgurr a'Fionn Choire but this is much harder. The view from Bruach na Frithe is superb. See Walk 25 for details.

It is also possible to make a direct ascent from Lota Corrie to Bruach na Frithe. Instead of turning right under the cliffs of Sgurr a'Fionn Choire as described above continue alongside the stream until it dwindles away. Keep on upwards over boulders and then scree to reach the ridge just east of the triangulation point. If descending this way keep left towards Sgurr a'Fionn Choire as there is a line of cliffs in the centre of the unnamed corrie lying south-east of Bruach na Frithe.

m There is an easy descent down boulders and scree from the Bealach nan Lice into grassy Fionn Choire (Fair Corrie). A spring at 2,690ft (890m) in the corrie is one of the highest water sources near the main ridge and very welcome on hot days.

n A path leaves the corrie and descends beside the burn to cross open moorland to the path from Sligachan to Glen Brittle across the low Bealach a'Mhaim. Turn right on this path and descend Coire na Circe beside the attractive Allt Dearg Mor with its many small waterfalls and deep pools back to Sligachan.

Bruach na Frithe (left), Sgurr a'Fionn Choire, Bealach nan Lice and Am Basteir from Sgurr Beag

DRUIM NAN RAMH

Druim nan Ramh is a long spur running south-east from the main Cuillin ridge separating Coruisk from Harta Corrie. The Coruisk face is a mass of slabs and crags with no easy way up for the walker. However the Harta Corrie slopes are much more broken and can be safely climbed in several places. The views from the ridge are superb.

a Walk down Glen Sligachan from Sligachan (see Walk 14) as far as the Lochan Dubha. Here leave the main path and turn right into Harta Corrie (see Walk 23).

START/FINISH:
Sligachan. There are places to park just before the A850 road crosses the bridge over the River Sligachan. There are good bus connections from Portree, Broadford and Kyle of Lochalsh with Citylink, Highland Country and Skye-Ways. There are even direct buses from Glasgow.

DISTANCE:
12 miles (20km)

APPROXIMATE TIME:
5–8 hours

HIGHEST POINT:
1,640ft (500m)

MAP:
Harveys Superwalker Skye: The Cuillin

REFRESHMENTS:
The Sligachan Hotel.

ADVICE:
The walk into Harta Corrie is easy but wet underfoot. The ascent of Druim nan Ramh is steep and rough and navigation could be difficult on the ridge in poor visibility.

On Druim nan Ramh with the northern Cuillin in the background

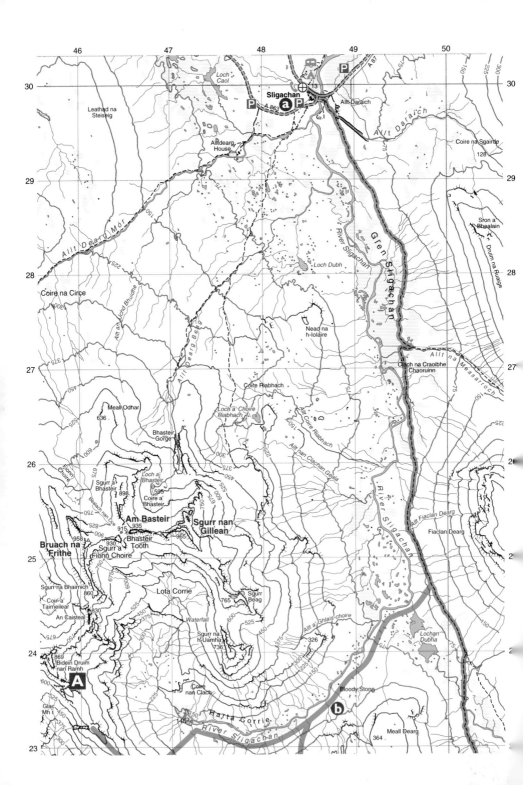

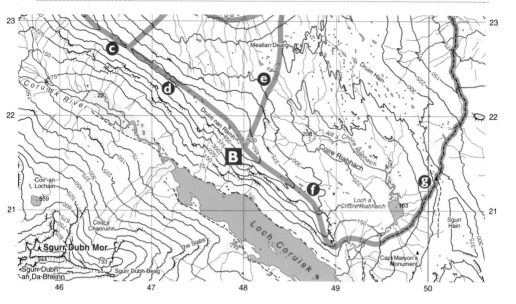

b Walk up the corrie beside the River Sligachan and past the great south face of Sgurr na h-Uamha. When the first water slides come into view a shallow dip can be seen up to the left on Druim nan Ramh. Ascend the steep slopes – boggy lower down, grassy and stony higher up – to this dip (467 227).

c From the dip you can head north-west towards Bidein Druim nan Ramh though after a short distance the terrain becomes quite difficult where a deep cleft cuts across the ridge with a rock tower called the Druim Pinnacle beyond it. Confident scramblers can climb in and out of the cleft and then edge round the pinnacle. The ascent of Bidein Druim nan Ramh from this point is a hard scramble however with sections of Moderate grade rock climbing. It is possible to skirt round the summit by following ledges leftwards to Bealach na Glaic Moire from where you can descend to Coruisk or Sligachan. Most walkers however will be content to gaze on the cliffs of Bidein Druim nan Ramh and then return along the ridge.

The northern Cuillin from Druim nan Ramh. From left: Sgurr a'Fionn Choire, Am Basteir, Sgurr nan Gillean and Sgurr na h-Uamha

A Bidein Druim nan Ramh 459 239

Druim nan Ramh means Ridge of the Oars, an unusual name. At the north-western end of the ridge lies 2,850ft-(869m-) Bidein Druim nan Ramh, the Sharp or Pointed Peak of the Ridge of Oars. While the walk along Druim nan Ramh is the easiest ridge walk in the Cuillin the ascent of Bidein Druim nan Ramh is one the hardest climbs despite it being one of the lowest summits on the main ridge. The peak has three summits of which the highest is the most difficult, the easiest route graded Moderate by rock climbers. It was first climbed in 1883 by Lawrence Pilkington (who also made the first ascent of the Inaccessible Pinnacle) along with Eustace Hulton and Horace Walker.

d Return to the dip from below Bidein Druim nan Ramh and follow the broad ridge south-east to the summit of Druim nan Ramh. The ridge is rough and rocky with many knolls, small lochans and patches of moss and grass. It's fairly level though and the walking is easy. In many places you can walk over rough gabbro slabs.

B Druim nan Ramh 480 217

There are wonderful views throughout the walk along Druim nan Ramh but those from the summit, a slight rise at the south-eastern end of the ridge, are particularly good. There are two small cairns on knolls of equal height here, one giving good views to the southern end of the ridge, one to the northern end. From the most southerly cairn Loch Coruisk lies below your feet with the southern end of the Cuillin ridge rising beyond it. All the peaks are impressive but none more so than Sgurr Dubh Mor (Big Black Peak), a dark wedge above massive cliffs with the long Dubh ridge running down from it to Loch Coruisk. The climb up this ridge – a Moderate grade rock climb – stretches for over 1 mile (1.6km) and ascends for almost 3,000ft (915m). It is said to be one of the finest ways up a mountain in the British Isles and according to the SMC District Guide is 'within reach of experienced scramblers with climbing ambitions'.

As well as Sgurr Dubh Mor the Inaccessible Pinnacle, seen end-on as a thin slice of rock, stands out. At the head of Coruisk lie Sgurr na Banachdich, Sgurr a'Ghreadaidh and Sgurr a'Mhadaidh, great peaks all but it's the vast sweeps of rock below the summits that attract the gaze. Out beyond Coruisk in the other direction Sgurr na Stri stands, small compared with the peaks on the ridge but still looking fine.

Turning north there is a tremendous view down to Harta Corrie from where the eye is led up to Lota Corrie and a ring of peaks from notched Bidein Druim nan Ramh at the far end of Druim nan Ramh over An Caisteal and Sgurr na Bhairnich, flat-topped Bruach na Frithe, Sgurr a'Fionn Chore, the Basteir Tooth and Am Basteir to the fine pointed summit of Sgurr nan Gillean and the huge pyramid of Sgurr na h-Uamha.

East of the last summit lies Glen Sligachan and Glamaig and the Red Hills with bulky Marsco almost blocking the end of Harta Corrie. But in this direction the peak that dominates the view is Bla Bheinn, a sensational wall of rock rising out of Srath na Creitheach.

Druim nan Ramh is hardly comparable to the high peaks of the Cuillin but it does have a small place in mountaineering history because the first recorded scramble took place here in 1835 when local ghillie Duncan MacIntyre (see Walk 28 for more of his exploits) and the Reverend Lesingham Smith returned to Sligachan from Coruisk over the ridge.

e A direct descent can be made from the summit back into Harta Corrie. Go north across the broad ridge for a few hundred yards then continue in the same direction down a steep grass, scree and rock gully. This leads to a broad shelf. Cross this then descend the final boggy slopes to the River Sligachan and the route back to Sligachan.

f A longer alternative route down is via the long south-east ridge. This is easy until you near the bottom where steep cliffs block the way. Go slightly left (north) here until you come to a gully with a burn in it that breaches the rocks. Descend the gully into lower Coire Riabhach just above Loch Coruisk.

g To return to Sligachan cross the burn running down the corrie to the path heading up the eastern side. This leads to the Druim Hain ridge and then down into Srath na Creitheach just south of the Lochan Dubha where it joins the main Camasunary-Sligachan path (see Walk 14 for more details).

Sgurr Dubh Mor from Druim nan Ramh

BRUACH NA FRITHE AND SGURR A'BHASTEIR

START/FINISH:
Sligachan. There are places
to park just before the A850
road crosses the bridge over
the River Sligachan. There
are good bus connections
from Portree, Broadford and
Kyle of Lochalsh with
Citylink, Highland Country
and Skye-Ways. There are
even direct buses from
Glasgow.

DISTANCE:
8 miles (13km)

APPROXIMATE TIME:
5–7 hours

HIGHEST POINT:
3,142ft (958m)

MAP:
Harveys Superwalker Skye:
The Cuillin

REFRESHMENTS:
The Sligachan Hotel.

ADVICE:
This is one of the easiest
walks in the Cuillin with only
mild scrambling involved.
However it still leads into
wild, remote country where
good route finding skills are
required, especially in poor
visibility as some of the
terrain is quite featureless.

Bruach na Frithe is a superb viewpoint and one of the easiest 3,000ft-(915m-) peaks in the Cuillin. It is set amongst savage rock scenery. Nearby Sgurr a'Bhasteir is also easy to climb and gives perhaps the best view of the Pinnacle Ridge of Sgurr nan Gillean.

a Begin a couple of hundred yards up the A863 road from Sligachan where a path sets off across the boggy moorland towards Sgurr nan Gillean. The path soon crosses the Allt Dearg Mor on a footbridge then continues climbing gently to the Allt Dearg Beag and another footbridge.

b Instead of crossing the second footbridge follow the path on the right (true left) bank of the burn. Ahead lies the deep gash of the Bhasteir Gorge with steep gabbro slabs rising either side of it.

c Approach the gorge but shortly before reaching the first slabs turn right (west), leaving the path, and climb to the bealach between the little spur of Meall Odhar and Sgurr a'Bhasteir.

d Ascend the north-north-west ridge of Sgurr a'Bhasteir. This is mostly walking on grass and rock with just a little easy scrambling.

Sgurr a'Bhasteir with Am Basteir
to the left

A Sgurr a'Bhasteir 464 257

Sgurr a'Bhasteir is a fine pyramid shaped peak that features in the classic view of Sgurr nan Gillean and Coire a'Bhasteir from Sligachan. It's on a spur running north from the main ridge, which makes it an excellent viewpoint for the spectacular rock wedge of Am Basteir hanging over the equally impressive Bhasteir Tooth and an even better one for the amazing Pinnacle Ridge of Sgurr nan Gillean. The summit is a narrow ridge with steep scree slopes on either side. A small cairn marks the highest point.

The east face of Bruach na Frithe

At 2,945ft (898m) Sgurr a'Bhasteir is below Munro level (3,000ft/915m) and therefore receives far less attention than higher peaks. The name is usually translated as Peak of the Executioner. The Executioner is nearby Am Basteir, so-called because of the resemblance of the Basteir Tooth to an axe. However Peter Drummond (Scottish Hill and Mountain Names) reckons Basteir may mean 'baptiser' or 'baptist', with the Tooth looking like the stooping, cowled head of a priest while the SMC District Guide to the Islands of Scotland says it possibly comes from a Gaelic word meaning cleft, presumably a description of the deep gash between Am Basteir and the Tooth.

B Am Basteir (466 253) and the Basteir Tooth (465 253)

These two huge blocks of rock dominate much of the views throughout the walk and their distinctive profile is clearly identifiable from afar. Both peaks are hard scrambles, the Tooth being particularly difficult, and should only be tackled by confident, experienced scramblers. For Am Basteir, the higher at 3,067ft (935m) and a Munro, the easiest ascent is along the east ridge from Bealach a'Bhasteir. The direct route involves a short but steep descent that is quite difficult, especially for those with a short reach. This drop has become much harder in recent years due to rockfall and requires rock-climbing skills. Cutting below the crest on the Lota Corrie (south) side when it begins to steepen is said to be easier as it avoids the descent, returning to the ridge at the gap below the drop. This way requires good route finding skills.

The Tooth cannot be ascended without some easy rock climbing. The only route even a competent scrambler can consider is one on the Lota Corrie side that follows a series of slanting gullies and grooves from the lowest point of the south face of Am Basteir across the face to the gap known as the Nick between An Basteir and the Tooth. From the Nick a slab can be climbed to the summit of the Tooth, an amazing

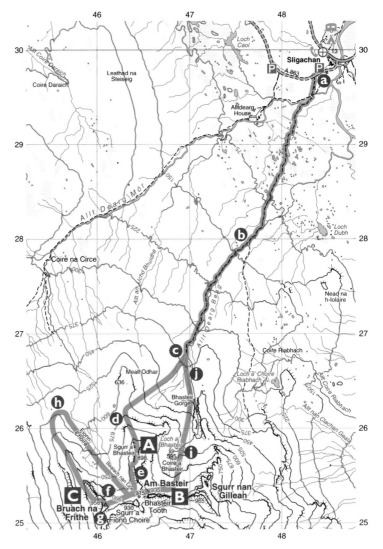

perch with sheer drops on three sides and the cliff of Am Basteir towering above on the other. This route can be reached by a scree path from the Bealach nan Lice. It was the route used by the first ascensionists of the Tooth, the famous partnership of local guide John Mackenzie and mountaineer Norman Collie, in 1889. Only rock climbers can make a direct link between Am Basteir and the Tooth.

e Descend the rocky south ridge of Sgurr a'Bhasteir, an easy walk, to join the main ridge at the Bealach nan Lice (Pass of the Flat Stones). Am Basteir and the Bhasteir Tooth grow more and more dramatic as you approach the bealach. When you reach the pass there is a superb view down into Lota Corrie.

f Turn right at the bealach and traverse below the crags of Sgurr a'Fionn Choire (scramblers can go over this top) to a slight dip above which rises the east ridge of Bruach na Frithe, from here a shapely pointed peak. The climb to the summit along the ridge is no more than a stony walk though there are some opportunities for scrambling along the way.

C   Bruach na Frithe 461 252

Bruach na Frithe is the only peak on the Cuillin ridge with a triangulation point. It's often said to be the easiest peak to climb on the ridge though Sgurr na Banachdich (see Walk 27) isn't any harder. The summit stands at a major change of direction on the ridge where it turns from east to west to north to south. The height is 3,142ft (958m), making Bruach na Frithe one of Skye's 12 Munros. The name means Slope (or Bank) of the Deer Forest or Wilderness. Bruach na Frithe was the second Cuillin summit to have a recorded ascent when it was climbed by local ghillie Duncan MacIntyre and the

Am Basteir and the Bhasteir Tooth

scientist Professor J.D. Forbes in 1845. They went on to climb the west ridge of Sgurr nan Gillean, a peak they had climbed by the south-east ridge two years earlier (see Walk 28 for more information).

East of the summit the huge rocky blocks of Am Basteir and the Bhasteir Tooth dominate the view, a wild, savage scene. To the south the rest of the Cuillin ridge twists and turns over a series of rocky peaks, an exciting and inspiring sight. Bla Bheinn is in view, a dark wedge to the south-east, with smaller Sgurr na Stri to its right and the Red Hills to its left. To the north-west is island-dotted Loch Bracadale with the Duirinish peninsula beyond it. The sea stacks of MacLeod's Maidens lie off the southern tip of Duirinish (see Walk 12) with the distinctive flat tops of MacLeod's Tables (see Walk 11) inland. Further round to the north Trotternish can be seen. And beyond Skye is the long dark undulating line of the Outer Hebrides, showing clearly why these islands are sometimes known as the Long Island.

g The easiest way down is to return to the Bealach nan Lice and descend into Fionn Choire and via the outward route to Sligachan. There are however exciting alternatives.

h Scramblers can descend the north-west ridge of Bruach na Frithe. The scrambling isn't difficult but there is one exposed section about halfway down. Generally the hardest scrambling is on the crest of the ridge and can be avoided on the left (west). The right side should be avoided, as there are steep cliffs here on the upper rim of Fionn Choire. Note that the rock is basalt and therefore slippery when wet. Around 2,300ft (700m) the scrambling ends and the ridge broadens and divides into two somewhat indistinct spurs with a shallow corrie between them. Take the spur to the right, which leads down into lower Fionn Choire where the path can be joined.

i The other option for the descent is to via spectacular Coire a'Bhasteir. For this return to the Bealach nan Lice and take a path that leads under the north face of the Bhasteir Tooth to scree slopes that lead down into the corrie. Alternatively the same path can be followed along the base of Am Basteir to the Bealach a'Bhasteir from where scree again leads down into the corrie.

C Coire a'Bhasteir 468 258
Coire a'Bhasteir is a dramatic corrie hidden from below by rock walls split by the Bhasteir Gorge and walled by the

tremendous skyline of Sgurr nan Gillean, Am Basteir, the Bhasteir Tooth and Sgurr a'Bhasteir. This is the classic view of the northern Cuillin, well seen from Sligachan. In the heart of the corrie is little Loch a'Bhasteir at a height of 1,952ft (595m). Cut off from the outside world and hard of access the heart of the corrie has the feeling of a secret world deep in the mountains. The Bhasteir Gorge is a deep, impressive ravine with sheer rock walls that was first climbed in 1890 by an Alpine Club party who had to swim across a 30ft- (10m-) pool at one point.

j   A cairned route leads out of Coire a'Bhasteir. This route works its way through the slabs high on the left (west) side of the Bhasteir Gorge where hands may be needed in a few places though it is a walk not a scramble. Care should be taken to follow the line of cairns. Once below the slabs follow the path beside the Allt Dearg Beag and the outward route back to Sligachan.

The Bhasteir Tooth

SGURR NA BANACHDICH AND SGURR NAN GOBHAR

START/FINISH:
Glen Brittle Youth Hostel.
Highland Country bus from
Portree via Sligachan twice a
day from mid-May to the
end of September.

DISTANCE:
4 miles (7km)

APPROXIMATE TIME:
4–6 hours

HIGHEST POINT:
3,165ft (965m)

MAP:
Harveys Superwalker Skye:
The Cuillin

REFRESHMENTS:
Small shop on Glen Brittle
campsite. Hotel at Sligachan.

ADVICE:
Steep scree has to be
climbed and there is some
easy scrambling if the
descent is made via Sgurr
nan Gobhar. Navigation can
be difficult in mist.

Sgurr na Banachdich is a fine peak in a dramatic setting. It's also a superb viewpoint, especially for Coruisk. The ascent via Coir'an Eich and An Diallaid is a walk rather than a scramble, and this is one of the easiest Cuillin peaks to climb.

a Opposite the Glen Brittle Youth Hostel a path sets out along the right (true left) bank of the Allt a'Choire Ghreadaidh. Take this path as far as the junction with the Allt Coir'an Eich.

b Continue up vegetated ground beside the Allt Coir'an Eich into Coir'an Eich (Corrie of the Horse), a small sloping corrie walled by steep scree.

c There are two different starts for the final climb to Sgurr na Banachdich from Coir'an Eich. Either go left and climb the scree to the spur called An Diallaid, which has three tiny tops and from where you can look down craggy slopes into large Coire a'Ghreadaidh. Walk along the spur, which soon reaches a small stony plateau where it merges with the broad western slopes of Sgurr na Banachdich, and climb scree and boulders to the summit. The alternative route goes more directly up the scree at the back of Coir'an Eich to the small plateau and the upper western slopes leading to the summit. There are several lines of cairns leading from the corrie to the summit and An Diallaid.

The east face of Sgurr na Banachdich

A   Sgurr na Banachdich 441 224

During the ascent Sgurr na Banachdich looks a somewhat shapeless broad dome composed mainly of scree so arriving at the summit is startling and dramatic as the narrow ridge falls away abruptly into Coireachan Ruadha to the east in a series of terraced cliffs. From the east Sgurr na Banachdich appears as a steep notched ridge with several summits above huge cliffs. Druim nan Ramh (Walk 24) and Sgurr na Stri (Walk 15) are two of the best viewpoints for this side of the mountain.

Sgurr na Banachdich is the easternmost Cuillin summit and also, at 3,165ft (965m), the easternmost Munro. It lies at about the centre of the main Cuillin ridge at a change in direction from north-west to north-east. To the south Sgurr Dearg (see Walk 29) rises as a huge dome with scree slopes on its western side and a steep broken craggy face to the east. The top of the Inaccessible Pinnacle can just be seen, poking above the rounded summit. Sgurr Alasdair and Sgurr Thearlaich appear, surprisingly, to the left of Sgurr Dearg. To the north rises the narrow crest of Sgurr a'Ghreadaidh with large Coire a'Ghreadaidh down to the left. Far below to the east lies Coruisk with its long dark loch and the little pyramid of Sgurr na Stri at its head. Beyond Coruisk rise Bla Bheinn and the Red Hills.

There are several possible meanings of Sgurr na Banachdich. One, reckoned unlikely by Peter Drummond (Scottish Hill and Mountain Names), is Smallpox Peak, from the Gaelic 'banachdaich', which could be a description of the pockmarked appearance of the rock though that could apply to any Cuillin peak. Drummond thinks the more likely meaning is Milkmaid's Peak, from the Gaelic for a milkmaid 'banaraich' or 'bananaich'. However D Noel Williams in the SMC District Guide to the Islands of Scotland gives other possibilities: vaccination from 'banachdach' or wasteland from 'ban-achadh'. Three of these meanings are of course linked, vaccination being discovered by the doctor and scientist Edward Jenner in 1796 after he noticed that people who caught the fairly harmless disease cowpox from cattle appeared to be immune to smallpox, which was usually fatal. He injected matter taken from a milkmaid who had cowpox into a boy who then developed the symptoms of cowpox. Later he injected the boy with smallpox and found he did not develop the disease due to the protection given him by having had cowpox.

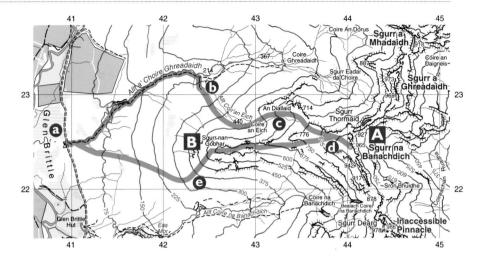

The peaks on the ridge either side of Sgurr na Banachdich can be reached by scramblers. Immediately to the north is small steep sided Sgurr Thormaid, which means Norman's Peak, after perhaps the greatest of the Cuillin pioneers Norman Collie. This is really the northern summit of Sgurr na Banachdich. To reach Sgurr Thormaid descend the north ridge of Sgurr na Banachdich, a moderate scramble, to a col sometimes called the Bealach Thormaid then climb the south-west ridge, a hard scramble, to the small exposed summit. Continuing on from here to the sensationally narrow summit ridge of Sgurr a'Ghreadaidh involves more hard exposed scrambling and is really only for the experienced. There are no descent routes for walkers or scramblers into Coire a'Ghreadaidh from Bealach Thormaid or the ridge north of Sgurr Thormaid. The only ways down are all rock climbs so it is necessary to return to Sgurr na Banachdich before descending.

South of the summit the narrow ridge drops for around ½ mile (800m) to the Bealach Coire na Banachdich at 2,791ft (851m). For the experienced this is an exciting scramble, quite exposed with big drops on the left (east) for much of its length and with some difficult sections, though these can be skirted on the right (west). Three tops are crossed during the descent of the ridge. These are the Centre Top, South Top and Sron Bhuidhe. From the bealach you can descend into Coire na Banachdich and pick up a path that leads back to Glen Brittle or continue up the steep scree of the north-west flank of Sgurr Dearg (see Walk 29). The descent into Coire na Banachdich isn't obvious though as steep slabs block the direct way down. Instead the route goes left from the bealach onto the northern scree slopes of Sgurr Dearg before descending slabs on the southern side of the corrie. This route is cairned but can still be hard to find in misty weather.

The first recorded ascent of Sgurr na Banachdich was in 1873 when it was climbed by the famous Cuillin pioneers John Mackenzie, a local guide, and Sheriff Alexander Nicolson along with Sgurr Dearg.

d For the non-scrambler the best descent route is to retrace the ascent route back to Coir'an Eich. A more interesting route is to follow the west ridge out to Sgurr nan Gobhar. This starts down the scree of the ascent route but instead of heading for An Diallaid when you reach the small plateau keep left onto the narrow ridge. The walk out to Sgurr nan Gobhar involves a little easy scrambling.

B Sgurr nan Gobhar 426 224

Little 2,066ft- (630m-) Sgurr nan Gobhar is the most easterly summit in the Cuillin and a good viewpoint for Glen Brittle, which lies directly below to the west. You can also look down into Coire na Banachdich and across to Sgurr Dearg as well as back to Sgurr na Banachdich. The name means Peak of the Goats.

e Crags encircle most of Sgurr nan Gobhar but on the south-western side there are extensive steep screes that can be descended. These screes make this a much better descent than ascent route as they are tedious and arduous to climb. Once down cross the boggy moor back to the start point.

Sgurr Dearg from Sgurr na Banachdich

GARS-BHEINN AND SGURR NAN EAG

START/FINISH:
Glen Brittle. Highland Country bus from Portree via Sligachan twice a day from mid-May to the end of September.

DISTANCE:
9 miles (15km)

APPROXIMATE TIME:
5–8 hours

HIGHEST POINT:
3,031ft (924m)

MAP:
Harveys Superwalker Skye: The Cuillin

REFRESHMENTS:
Small shop on Glen Brittle campsite. Hotel at Sligachan.

ADVICE:
Although mostly walking some easy scrambling is required. Navigation can be difficult in mist. The lower slopes can be very wet.

Sgurr nan Eag and Gars-bheinn are the southernmost peaks on the Cuillin ridge. Both are good viewpoints, especially south and west over the sea. This walk passes through magnificent Coir'a'Ghrundda, which contains the highest loch in the Cuillin. The ridge between Bealach a'Garbh-choire and Gars-bheinn is the longest section of the main ridge easily accessible to the walker, a superb high level route.

A   Glen Brittle 409 206
Glen Brittle lies at the end of a long winding single-track road that runs from the B8009 near Carbost. There are tremendous views of the Cuillin ridge where the road crests the boggy moorland ridge separating Glen Drynoch from Glen Brittle. Glen Brittle has a youth hostel, a climber's hut and a campsite and is the centre for ventures onto the southern half of the Cuillin ridge. Below the road end near the campsite lies the beach, a long strip of black sand popular with waders and other shore birds.

a   To reach the start of the walk go through the campsite and over the fence just past the toilet block. Cross the track to Rubh' an Dunain (see Walk 6) and climb slowly west on a path through boggy moorland. After almost ½ mile (800m) the path forks. Leave the main path, which continues east into Coire Lagan, and take the right fork.

View south over Soay to Eigg and Rum

The rocky mouth of upper Coir'a'Ghrundda with the Caisteal a'Garbh-Choire on the horizon

b The path crosses a stream and makes a gently rising traverse towards the broad south-west slopes of Sron na Ciche. Just before the foot of Sron na Ciche the path crosses the Allt Coire Lagan. There are two parallel paths beyond the burn. The upper is the one to take, the lower will be used on the return.

c The path hugs the base of Sron na Ciche and curves round crags at the southern end of this peak into lower Coir'a'Ghrundda. Huge cliffs rise on your left, the North and South Crags of Sron na Ciche. The cairned route stays high on the left side of the lower corrie threading a way through boulders well above the rounded ice-smoothed boilerplate slabs in the centre of the corrie. A great wall of these slabs curves down from the lip of the upper corrie, an apparently impregnable barrier. The path heads for the waterfall where the Allt Coir'a'Ghrundda crashes down from the upper corrie. Just to the left of the falls a slanting groove in the rock provides a surprisingly easy scramble through the slabs and into the upper corrie.

A   Coir'a'Ghrundda 451 202
Upper Coir'a'Ghrundda is a tremendous bowl, hemmed in by huge rock walls topped by rocky peaks. A large loch fills much of this classic glaciated hanging valley. What is not water is stone, hence the corrie's name, which means the Bare Corrie. Yet despite the harshness and lack of vegetation this is an idyllic, magical place, a secret haven in the heart of the mountains. The cliffs and steep scree and boulder slopes rising up on three sides dominate the scene. The peaks themselves are too close, the view of them too foreshortened, to stand out.

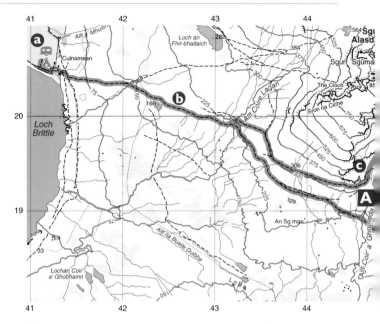

d Cross the corrie to the south-east corner of the loch then climb the steep, rocky slopes above to the main Cuillin ridge at the Bealach a'Garbh-choire at 2,614ft (797m). This ascent is arduous but no real scrambling is involved though hands may be useful at times.

B Bealach a'Garbh-choire 454 203
The bealach lies at the foot of a huge block of rough peridotite rock, the 2,716ft- (828m-) Caisteal a'Garbh-choire (Castle of the Rough Corrie). Rock climbing skills are required to climb this edifice. To the east lies Garbh-choire, a chaotic tangle of boulders and rock tumbling down into Coruisk. It is possible to descend this corrie but the going is very rough.

There are paths along the base of both sides of the Caisteal a'Garbh-choire and an easy ascent can be made from the north side to 3,077ft- (938m-) Sgurr Dubh na Da Bheinn (Black Peak of the Two Ridges). This peak sits at the junction of the Dubh ridge that runs all the way down to Coruisk and the main Cuillin ridge, hence the name. It's a subsidiary peak of 3,096ft- (944m-) Sgurr Dubh Mor (the Big Black Peak), which lies a short way along the Dubh ridge. The scramble to this summit is quite hard and exposed in places and not for the inexperienced.

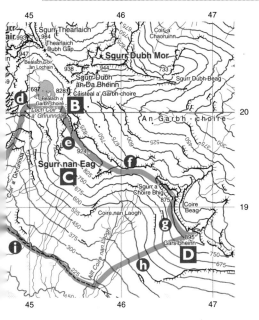

e From the bealach head south along the ridge to Sgurr nan Eag. This involves scrambling if you stay on the crest of the ridge but all difficulties can be avoided on the Coir' a'Ghrundda (west) side where there are paths across the scree. The 1,300ft- (400m-) long summit ridge has three small tops, the third, at the far south-eastern end of the ridge, being the highest.

C   Sgurr nan Eag 456 196

Sgurr nan Eag is a huge mountain, forming the craggy south-west wall of An Garbh-choire and with vast scree and rock slopes falling away to Coir' a'Ghrundda to the south-west. The peak can be climbed fairly easily via these slopes but it's a long, arduous ascent and nowhere near as interesting as the approach via the Bealach a'Garbh-choire.

The view is excellent and wide-ranging. To the south the islands of Rum and Eigg stand out, while to the west the Outer Hebrides can be seen. To the south-east the final twists and turns of the Cuillin ridge lead down to Gars-bheinn. More dramatic is the view north to Sgurr Dubh Mor and Sgurr Alasdair. From the north-western end of the summit ridge you can look straight down to Loch Coir' a'Ghrundda, an amazing view. Eastwards lie the rocky depths of An Garbh-choire running down to Loch Coruisk with the long Dubh ridge on the far side.

Gars-bheinn (left), Sgurr a'Choire Bhig, Sgurr nan Eag, Caisteal a'Garbh-choire, Sgurr Dubl na Da Bheinn and Sgurr Dubh Mor

The name means Notched Peak, a reference to the gaps or slots in the mountain visible from afar.

f A fine ridge walk leads from Sgurr nan Eag over 2,870ft- (875m-) Sgurr a'Choire Bhig (Peak of the Little Corrie – Coire Beag lies to the south-east) to the final peak on the Cuillin ridge 2,936ft- (895m-) Gars-bheinn. Throughout there are excellent views of Loch Coruisk and Soay and Cuillin Sounds. The walk starts with a 500ft- (150m-) descent. There are scrambling opportunities on the edge of An Garbh-choire, though these can easily be avoided on the right (south) side.

g A 360ft- (110m-) climb leads up the north-west ridge to the summit of Sgurr a'Choire Bhig. Initially the ridge is broad and boulder-covered with one large flat section. Above this the ridge narrows and the walk along the crest is exciting if a little exposed. There is a path down to the right (west) that is less airy. There is an excellent view of the Dubh ridge from the summit, which is made from basalt rather than gabbro. Next descend the south ridge of Sgurr a'Choire Bhig, which involves some easy scrambling at the start. This leads to a dip at 2,722ft (830m) after which there is an easy walk to the summit of Gars-bheinn. This goes over two minor tops before the summit is reached. The scree gullies seen on the left here run down into remote, little-visited Coire Beag.

D   Gars-bheinn 468 187

The southernmost summit of the Cuillin is a dramatic viewpoint. To the south there are no mountains, just a vast expanse of sea and sky. In the distance lie the islands of Rum and Eigg with the Western Highlands to their left. To the north the ridge stretches out, a long snaking line of rippling rocky peaks. Most of the main summits can be seen.

The summit is quite large and there are a number of low stone walls ringing some of the ledges. These mark bivouac sites used by climbers before they set out on a traverse of the whole ridge. The name may mean Echoing Hill, though this seems uncertain.

h   The most interesting return route is to back the way you have come. Those who prefer a circular route can descend the vast loose scree and boulder slopes south-west of Gars-bheinn. This is an arduous way down though nothing like as hard or tedious as ascending the scree. After some 1,650ft (500m) the rock fades away to be replaced by boggy moorland. Continue across this in the same direction until you reach a path traversing the hillside at around 740ft (225m). This is the continuation of the lower path below Sron na Ciche (see b above).

i   Turn right on the path and follow it back across the moorland to rejoin the outward route at the Allt Coire Lagan.

Sgurr Sgumain and Sgurr Alasdair rising out of mist in Coir'a Ghrundda

SGURR NAN GILLEAN

START/FINISH:
Sligachan. There are places to park just before the A850 road crosses the bridge over the River Sligachan. There are good bus connections from Portree, Broadford and Kyle of Lochalsh with Citylink, Highland Country and Skye-Ways, and direct buses from Glasgow.

DISTANCE:
7 miles (12km)

APPROXIMATE TIME:
5–8 hours

HIGHEST POINT:
3,165ft (965m) Sgurr nan Gillean

MAP:
Harveys Superwalker Skye: The Cuillin

REFRESHMENTS:
The Sligachan Hotel.

ADVICE:
The ascent of Sgurr nan Gillean is the most difficult route in the book. The final climb to the summit involves hard, exposed scrambling, making this a walk for the experienced scrambler. Navigation can be difficult in mist. The lower sections can be wet and muddy.

Sgurr nan Gillean is one of the most magnificent peaks in the Cuillin, a soaring pyramid buttressed by pinnacled ridges. Rising south of Sligachan it is a well-known, much photographed peak. The ascent is mostly a walk, except for the last hard scramble up the south-east ridge. This is known, misleadingly, as the Tourist Route. The summit is small and airy with a superb view.

a The walk begins just across the road from the Sligachan Hotel where a path runs a few hundred yards to a bridge over the Allt Dearg Mor (Big Red Burn) and a fork in the path. The path following the stream to the right here leads to the Bealach a'Mhaim and Glen Brittle. Cross the bridge and take the path on the far side across wet and boggy moorland to another stream, the Allt Dearg Beag (Little Red Burn), a beautiful stream of little waterfalls and deep pools. The path heads upstream a short way to another bridge and another fork in the path. Here the path on the right following the stream leads into Coire a'Bhasteir. Our path continues across the bridge and over the flat shoulder of Nead na h-Iolaire (the Eagle's Nest) to Coire Riabhach (Streaked or Grey Corrie).

b There is a slight descent then the path crosses the western slopes of the corrie, high above Loch a'Choire Riabhach, before climbing scree and then rocks to flat stony slopes on the eastern side of Sgurr nan Gillean. This leads

The Pinnacle ridge of Sgurr nan Gillean

into a small corrie called Coire nan Allt Geala that is littered with little crags, boulders and rocks. The huge towers of Pinnacle Ridge rise directly above the path here.

c   The cairned route crosses the corrie then curves right to ascend a gully up the craggy back wall. This leads to bouldery slopes up which the route zigzags to the ridge between Sgurr Beag and Sgurr nan Gillean from where the south-east ridge soars up steeply to the summit, an awe inspiring and somewhat intimidating sight.

d   Turn right on the ridge and begin the ascent of the south-east ridge of Sgurr nan Gillean. The scrambling is fairly easy at first as difficulties can be avoided on the left, Lota Corrie, side. Higher up the ridge begins to narrow though and route choices become limited. It gets steeper too and more exposed. The final 100ft (30m) are the hardest. Here you have to either climb the very narrow ridge directly or skirt it on steep sloping rocks on the left. Both ways are exposed and have some awkward moves. Before going up this last section note that it will also have to be descended. Some walkers will probably decide this is far enough. And all but very experienced confident scramblers may well want the protection of a rope. The final few yards to the tiny summit are very airy.

The south-east ridge of Sgurr nan Gillean

A   Sgurr nan Gillean 472 253

The summit of Sgurr nan Gillean is a tiny platform at the apex of three ridges. So steep are these that you can't see them from the summit, which gives a strange and exciting feeling of hanging in the air. If you scramble a little way down from the summit you can look down on Knight's Peak, the last and highest top on Pinnacle Ridge, and also down the west ridge. Unsurprisingly, the views from the summit are excellent and extensive. To the south-west the Cuillin ridge sweeps round in a huge arc split by the long ridge of Druim nan Ramh. Below your feet lies Lota Corrie with Harta Corrie beyond it. In the other direction lies Sligachan and Loch Sligachan stretching out to Raasay. Much further north the distinctive Trotternish ridge can be seen. East, across Glen Sligachan, are the rounded Red Hills. South of them rise Garbh-bheinn and mighty Bla Bheinn, looking very imposing even from this high vantage point.

Despite being one of the most difficult summits Sgurr nan Gillean was one of the first to be climbed, presumably because it is such a distinctive peak. The ascent was made in

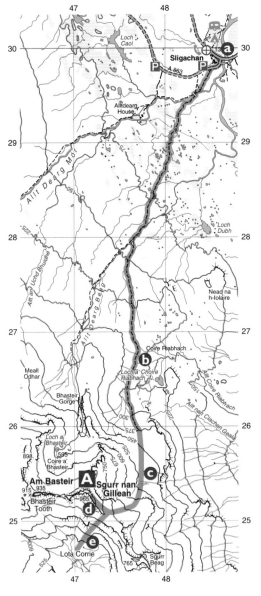

1836, long before mountaineering existed as a pursuit for its own sake, by local ghillie Duncan MacIntyre, who had already made several attempts on the peak, and J.D. Forbes, Professor of Natural Philosophy at Edinburgh University. They climbed the south-east ridge, a route picked out by MacIntyre. Before the ascent many regarded Sgurr nan Gillean, along with the rest of the Cuillin, as unclimbable.

At the time of the first ascent Sgurr nan Gillean was reckoned the highest peak in the Cuillin but Forbes wasn't convinced of this, saying that 'Sgurr-na-panachtich' (Sgurr na Banachdich) appeared to be as high. He was right, there only being 1ft (30cm) difference between the two peaks. And at 3,165ft (965m) Sgurr nan Gillean is in fact the fifth highest peak in the Cuillin.

In 1845 Forbes returned to the Cuillin and again climbed Sgurr nan Gillean with Duncan MacIntyre, this time from the west, having climbed Bruach na Frithe first. Forbes carried a barometer so he could measure the heights of the summits, something that had never been done before. By comparing his readings with ones made in Portree at the same time he worked out that Sgurr nan Gillean was 'between 3,200 and 3,220ft' and Bruach na Frithe 'about 40ft lower'. Forbes was some 35ft out, very accurate given the methods used.

On the same visit to the Cuillin Forbes made the first circumnavigation of the range and then compiled the first reasonably accurate map of the Cuillin including heights for the summits. No better map appeared until the first Ordnance Survey one 40 years later.

Forbes also made the first geological survey of the mountains, showing that glaciers had existed in the Cuillin. He had previously studied glaciation in the Alps, making the first accurate map of the Mer de Glace on Mont Blanc. He also climbed the Stockhorn in the Valais region, the first British ascent of an unclimbed Alpine peak, and later the Jungfrau, both major mountaineering feats for the time.

Though he always had a scientific reason for his explorations Forbes can be regarded as the precursor to later Cuillin pioneers such as Alexander Nicolson and Norman Collie. Ian Mitchell describes him as 'a hairsbreadth from being a mountaineer' (Scotland's Mountains Before The Mountaineers). When he died in 1868 no ascents other than his and MacIntyre's of Sgurr nan Gillean and Bruach na Frithe had been made in the Cuillin.

Although he gave no details Forbes' second ascent of Sgurr nan Gillean was almost certainly by the west ridge. The main barrier on this ridge was a huge pinnacle known as the Gendarme, which blocked the ridge, forcing climbers to edge round its overhanging sides. However in 1987 this collapsed. The ridge is still very exposed and narrow and is a rock climb, graded Moderate. A less exposed though harder alternative is via Nicolson's Chimney, first descended by Alexander Nicolson in 1865, in the company of Duncan MacIntyre's son, though it was 1879 before he made the first ascent. Today the chimney is graded Difficult.

The third ridge of Sgurr nan Gillean, Pinnacle Ridge, is a much more serious proposition. It's graded Moderate but the climbing sections are much more sustained and one abseil is involved.

Sgurr nan Gillean means either Peak of the Young Men or Peak of the Gullies. No explanation for the first meaning is apparent but if the second is correct it may come from the Norse 'gil' meaning a gully.

e   For walkers and scramblers the only possible descent route is back down the south-east ridge. The return to Sligachan could then be made via Lota and Harta Corries or by An Glas-choire (see Walk 23) but either of these would mean a long walk out down Glen Sligachan.

SGURR DEARG

START/FINISH:
Glen Brittle Memorial Hut. Highland Country bus from Portree via Sligachan twice a day from mid-May to the end of September.

DISTANCE:
5 miles (8km)

APPROXIMATE TIME:
4–7 hours

HIGHEST POINT:
3,208ft (978m) Sgurr Dearg

MAP:
Harveys Superwalker Skye: The Cuillin

REFRESHMENTS:
Small shop on Glen Brittle campsite. Hotel at Sligachan.

ADVICE:
Although short this is a steep route with much scree to climb and descend. The short sections of scrambling are easy. The navigation however can be tricky, especially in mist.

Sgurr Dearg lies on the Cuillin ridge between two fine corries, Coire na Banachdich and Coire Lagan. The highest point on the mountain is the amazing fang of rock known as the Inaccessible Pinnacle, the most difficult 3,000-ft peak in the Cuillin. This walk ascends Coire na Banachdich, passing the longest waterfall in the Cuillin on the way, climbs Sgurr Dearg and then descends magnificent Coire Lagan.

a   The walk starts in Glen Brittle between the Memorial Hut, a climber's hut run jointly by the British Mountaineering Council and the Mountaineering Council of Scotland, and Glenbrittle House. A path heads east here, past some sheep pens, and after a few hundred yards reaches the Allt Coire na Banachdich just below a water pipe. Cross the burn on a footbridge and follow the path uphill to the rim of a huge bowl where the burn crashes down in a long waterfall, the Eas Mor.

A   Eas Mor 420 212
The Eas Mor (Great Waterfall) is a tremendous waterfall tumbling unbroken some 80ft (24m) down sheer cliffs into a deep pool in a birch filled gorge. The roar of the falls can be heard from many places in Glen Brittle. Louis Stott in The Waterfalls of Scotland calls it 'the grandest mountain fall in Skye'.

b   Just above Eas Mor the path forks. Stay left here, beside the burn. The right fork goes to Coire Lagan and will be used on the descent. The path stays by the burn, rounds the foot of Window Buttress at the end of the west ridge of Sgurr Dearg and reaches the mouth of Coire na Banachdich. Here it leaves the burn and heads directly up the stony slopes of the corrie towards the headwall.

c   The headwall of the corrie consists of steep slabs split by a big gully (Banachdich Gully – a rock climb graded Very Difficult). To avoid the crags the path heads right towards Sgurr Dearg and zigzags up slabs on the left (true right) side of the burn, which here runs in a deep gorge. An easy scree gully takes you above the crags where the route cuts back left up a broad rocky terrace to the bealach. The way is cairned throughout but can still be difficult to locate in mist, especially in descent.

B   Bealach Coire na Banachdich 443 218

A bump of rock marks 2,792ft- (851m-) Bealach Coire na Banachdich, the easiest pass between Glen Brittle and Coruisk. To the north the south ridge of Sgurr na Banachdich rises, a moderate scramble with some exposure. The blunt spur of Sron Bhuidhe (Yellow Nose) juts out from the lower ridge into Coireachan Ruadh (Red Corrie) whose scree slopes run down into Coruisk. To the south Sgurr Dearg rises as a huge dome, the dark north face a mass of steep crags and overhangs.

d   From the bealach follow a cairned path up the scree covered northern slopes of Sgurr Dearg. There are good views of the north face during the ascent.

C Sgurr Dearg 444 216

The summit of Sgurr Dearg is a thin ridge of rock set high above Coire Lagan. It's an amazing situation because just below it to the east rises the fantastic fin of rock called the Inaccessible Pinnacle. This overtops the summit of Sgurr Dearg by 26ft (8m) and so is the true top of the mountain. It's also, at 3,234ft (986m), the second highest summit on Skye after Sgurr Alasdair and a Munro. While Sgurr Dearg is easy to climb the Inaccessible Pinnacle is very difficult, the hardest Munro by far. The easiest route is via the East Ridge, a sensationally exposed Moderate grade rock climb. On climbing it you can easily understand the Victorian hyperbole

The Inaccessible Pinnacle and Sgurr Dearg

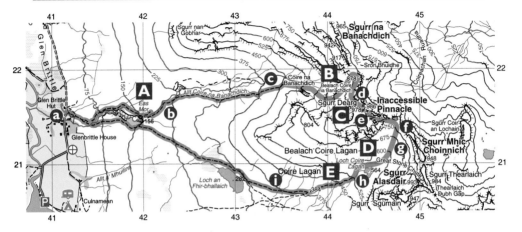

that it has an 'overhanging and infinite drop on one side and a drop longer and steeper on the other'. It does in fact drop some 2,000ft (600m) into Coireachan Ruadha on the north side. In places the East Ridge is less than 1ft (30cm) wide and the sides are sheer. The climbing isn't difficult. There are plenty of large hand and foot holds. It's the drops either side that are overwhelming. The summit is a small sloping platform dotted with a few large boulders. The descent is by an abseil down the West Ridge. Non-rock climbers require an experienced leader, a rope and a great deal of nerve before they can attempt the climb. Munro baggers will want to do this. Other walkers may well be content to sit on the summit of Sgurr Dearg and watch others make the ascent.

Oddly, in the original Tables, published in the Scottish Mountaineering Club Journal in 1891, Sir Hugh Munro listed the Inaccessible Pinnacle as a subsidiary Top and Sgurr Dearg as the Munro even though he correctly listed the former as being the higher of the two. This was corrected in the second edition of the Tables, published in 1921 after Munro's death but based largely on his notes. Munro never actually climbed the Inaccessible Pinnacle, one of the few summits in his Tables he didn't ascend.

Whilst the Inaccessible Pinnacle dominates the summit of Sgurr Dearg there is also a superb view across Coire Lagan to Sgurr Alasdair and Sgurr Thearlaich with the long pale ribbon of the Great Stone Chute between them (see Walk 30).

Sgurr Dearg was first climbed, along with Sgurr na Banachdich, in 1873 by Alexander Nicolson and Angus Macrae, a local shepherd, but they didn't attempt the

Inaccessible Pinnacle, Nicolson later writing that 'it might be possible, with ropes and grappling irons, to overcome it; but the achievement seems hardly worth the trouble.' The first ascent came in 1880 when the East Ridge was climbed by Lawrence and Charles Pilkington, of glass making fame, who were two of the leading mountaineers of the day. John Mackenzie is believed to have made the second ascent a year later. Five years after that W.P. Haskett Smith, famous for the first ascent of Napes Needle on Great Gable in the English Lake District, went up and down the East Ridge in just twelve minutes. In the same year two climbers called Stocker and Parker made the first ascent of the West Ridge and then descended the East Ridge for the first traverse. John Mackenzie and R.C. Broomfield repeated this soon afterwards. Inaccessible no more the Pinnacle is now climbed hundreds of times every year by both Munroists and those traversing the Cuillin ridge with queues building up at times in the summer.

The name Inaccessible Pinnacle was bestowed on the peak by the first surveyors and mountaineers in the mid-19th century. Before that it was known as An Stac, from the Norse word 'stakkr' meaning steep, a name now used for a minor top lower down on the south-east ridge of Sgurr Dearg. This can be easily climbed by descending along the south side of the Inaccessible Pinnacle and then walking along the ridge to the summit, which is a superb viewpoint for the East Ridge.

e   The top of Sgurr Dearg can be confusing in mist as a rib of slabs runs across the line of the ridge just a few feet below the ridge. Care needs to be taken to cross rather than follow this rib as it finishes on the edge of the cliffs of the north face.

f   The easiest way back to the start is to return to Coire na Banachdich. However it is much more interesting and only slightly more difficult and a little longer to descend via Coire Lagan. In mist the route finding can be difficult though and great care must be taken to keep to the correct line as there are steep cliffs all around.

g   Begin the descent to Coire Lagan by going down rough slopes from Sgurr Dearg to the base of the Inaccessible Pinnacle then following a broad stony ramp below the south face of the Pinnacle to the foot of the East Ridge. Stay with the ramp as it runs below the southern slopes of An Stac to a cairn by some boulders where the route turns left to the Bealach Coire Lagan. Steep scree slopes run down towards

Coire Lagan here. It is very important not to descend these. They lead to a sheer drop that can't be seen from above.

D   Bealach Coire Lagan 447 215

Bealach Coire Lagan is the low point on the headwall of Coire Lagan. Despite the name it's not usually used as a pass between Glen Brittle and Coruisk as the slopes on the latter side are very steep and loose.

Beyond the bealach the main ridge runs south across a flat area to the lowest point on the corrie wall and the north ridge of 3,109ft- (948m-) Sgurr Mhic Choinnich. The ascent of this peak involves moderate scrambling along a knife-edge basalt crest with much exposure. The top is fairly roomy but beyond lies a sheer drop, the easiest way up which is a Difficult graded rock climb. Scramblers can go no further. The first ascent of Sgurr Mhic Choinnich was made by a party led by Charles Pilkington in 1884.

Sgurr Mhic Chonnich was named in honour of John Mackenzie (Mhic Choinnich in Gaelic). Mackenzie was an astonishing character, a local man who climbed Sgurr nan Gillean solo at the age of ten. Then at 14 he made the first ascent of Sgurr a'Ghreadiadh, a difficult and exposed scramble, along with 15 year old W.N. Tribe, who later became a leading mountaineer. Mackenzie became a mountain guide and climbed regularly with Norman Collie in a career that stretched over 50 years.

The west face of Sgurr Mhic Choinnich forms the vast headwall of Coire Lagan. From the corrie below figures can sometimes be seen apparently levitating across this face. They are in fact walking and scrambling along a surprisingly wide ledge that traverses the face from end to end. This is Collie's Ledge, after Norman Collie who was believed to have made the first crossing of it with John Mackenzie. However Noel Williams in Skye Scrambles says that it had been climbed a year earlier by an Irish climber called Henry Hart along with John Mackenzie and so should be called Hart's Ledge. In that case though why not call it Mackenzie's Ledge, especially as it lies on his mountain and he was on the first and second crossing. The scramble along the ledge isn't difficult but the situation is sensational. The ledge starts on the north-west ridge, slants across the face and then descends a short way to the Bealach Mhic Choinnich, a narrow gap between the steep rocky crags of Sgurr Mhic Choinnich and Sgurr Thearlaich. The final descent is the hardest part of the route. From Bealach Mhic Choinnich scree slopes can be descended to the lower part of the Great Stone Chute (see Walk 30).

h   From the Bealach Coire Lagan steep screes, known as the An Stac screes, run down into Coire Lagan. The descent of these isn't difficult. The ascent is very hard work, which is why this walk is best done this way round.

E   Coire Lagan 445 209

Coire Lagan is a beautiful bowl set in the wild heart of the highest mountains on Skye. A fine lochan lies in the centre of the corrie in a basin of huge boilerplate slabs. After the exertions on the heights it's a wonderful to rest and look back up to the steep cliffs and scree slopes above. The name means Corrie of the Hollow.

i   A path leaves the north-east corner of the corrie and descends rocky slopes to the open moor below the corrie. Watch for a right fork heading for Loch an Fhir-bhallaich (Lake of the Speckled Trout) and take this past the loch and over the moor below Window Buttress to the Eas Mor and the start. The path continuing straight down to the south of the loch leads to the Glen Brittle campsite. This could be taken and the road then followed back to the start.

The Inaccessible Pinnacle

SGURR ALASDAIR

START/FINISH:
Glen Brittle campsite.
Highland Country bus from
Portree via Sligachan twice a
day from mid-May to the
end of September.

DISTANCE:
5 miles (8km)

APPROXIMATE TIME:
5–7 hours

HIGHEST POINT:
3,257ft (993m)

MAP:
Harveys Superwalker Skye:
The Cuillin

REFRESHMENTS:
Small shop on Glen Brittle
campsite. Hotel at Sligachan.

ADVICE:
Although short in distance
this walk involves a great
deal of steep ascent, much
of it on scree. At the very top
there is a short section of
moderate scrambling.

Sgurr Alasdair is the highest peak in the Cuillin and a wonderful viewpoint. The climb to this fine pointed peak goes through beautiful Corrie Lagan and up the long slopes of the Great Stone Chute.

a   The walk starts at the south-east corner of the Glen Brittle campsite where the path to Corrie Lagan starts just past the toilet block. The path climbs boggy moorland towards the Coire Lagan skyline.

b   The path passes Loch an Fhir-bhallaich on the left. Just beyond the loch there are forks to the left and right. Stay with the main path, which heads east below the slopes of Window Buttress. In lower Corrie Lagan the ground starts to steepen and the moor is left behind for stony slopes that lead to the rim of impressive upper Coire Lagan.

A   Sron na Ciche 448 204
As you climb towards Coire Lagan a long, high ridge is visible to the south. This is Sron na Ciche. The cliffs on its north face are the biggest in the Cuillin, some ½ mile (800m) long and nearly 1,000ft (30m) high, and a popular destination for rock climbers. A major feature is a massive lump of rock protruding outwards from the centre of the cliffs. This was first discovered by the great Cuillin climber Norman Collie. He

Sgurr Alasdair and the Great Stone Chute

noticed a large shadow on the face of Sron na Ciche when descending Coire Lagan in 1899 though it was 1906 before he followed this up and made the first ascent with John Mackenzie. It was Mackenzie who named the huge rock A'Chioch (the breast), after which Sron na Ciche, the Nose of the Breast, takes its name. The easiest routes on the Sron na Ciche cliffs are Moderate grade rock climbs. A very experienced scrambler could tackle these. There are no routes for walkers.

The north end of Sron na Ciche is separated from the next summit, Sgurr Sgumain, by the Bealach Coir'a'Ghrundda. The Sgumain Stone Shoot, a mixture of large rocks and scree, runs up to this pass, which can be used to reach Coir'a'Ghrundda from Coire Lagan.

B Sgurr Sgumain 448 207
The south-west ridge of Sgurr Alasdair runs out to a broad blocky top. This is Sgurr Sgumain (Stack Peak), a name once given to the whole Sgurr Alasdair ridge. The north-west face hanging over Coire Lagan is very impressive. From the top of the Sgumain Stone Shoot it's just a walk to the summit of Sgurr Sgumain. Continuing on to Sgurr Alasdair is a much more difficult proposition however. The scramble down to the Bealach Sgumain isn't too hard but the ascent of the south-west ridge of Sgurr Alasdair involves a hard scramble. There is a bad step on this ridge that requires a few rock climbing moves but this can be avoided by a well-used chimney on the Coir'a'Ghrundda side.

Sgurr Alasdair and Loch Coire'a'Ghrundda

c Walk past the lochan in upper Coire Lagan then head right to the foot of the Great Stone Chute, an unmistakable fan of scree. Climb the 1,300ft- (400m-) Chute, an arduous and sometimes frustrating task. The best line is probably on the edges where the rocks are slightly more stable than the small scree in the centre. Halfway up rock walls close in around the Chute. This narrower section is very eroded with much bare rock showing. The easiest going is next to the walls. Beware of stones knocked down from parties above and try not to dislodge rocks onto anyone below you. As the Chute curves you may not see other climbers above you so don't assume it's safe because no-one is in sight.

C Top of the Great Stone Chute
The top of the Great Stone Chute is a narrow col with Sgurr Thearlaich on the left (east) and Sgurr Alasdair on the right (west). This col is not a pass. The screes descending into

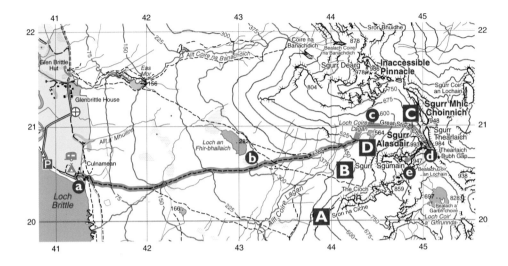

Coir'a'Ghrundda end at the top of a cliff. On the descent ensure you go the right way here, which is north.

Sgurr Thearlaich, the north-east top of Sgurr Alasdair, is a hard scramble, the easiest start being a short way down on the Coir'a'Ghrundda side of the col. Thearlaich is the Gaelic for Charles and the peak is named for Charles Pilkington who led the first ascent in 1887.

d From the col a short, steep scramble up basalt rocks leads to the summit of Sgurr Alasdair.

Evening light over the Coire Lagan skyline with Sgurr Alasdair in the centre

Sgurr Alasdair and Loch
Coire'a'Ghrundda

D Sgurr Alasdair 450 208
The highest point on Skye is tiny and airy with steep slopes on
every side, a magnificent situation. The views are superb.
Sgurr Dearg and the Inaccessible Pinnacle stand out high
above the depths of Coire Lagan. However the real glory is in
the tremendous seascape to the south and west with the Inner
and Outer Isles visible in a vast expanse of sea. To the south-
west a mass of mainland peaks can be seen.

Sgurr Alasdair is named for Alexander Nicolson, Alasdair
being the Gaelic for Alexander, who made the first ascent in
1873 with shepherd Angus Macrae, having already climbed
Sgurr na Banachdich and Sgurr Dearg the same day. Nicolson
called the peak Scur a Laghain. At the time Sgurr Dearg was
thought to be the highest peak in the Cuillin. It was 1887
before Norman Collie discovered Sgurr Alasdair was the true
high point and it was named in honour of Nicolson.

Nicolson was a native of Skye who had left the island to
become in turn a university lecturer, a journalist and
newspaper editor and a lawyer before finishing as a sheriff
first in Kirkcudbright then Greenock.

e   The only way down from Sgurr Alasdair for the walker is
via the Great Stone Chute. Confident scramblers can descend
the south-west ridge and continue over Sgurr Sgumain to the
Sgumain Stone Shoot, which leads down into Coire Lagan
(see B above).

FACT FILE

TOURIST INFORMATION

Portree, Bayfield House, Bayfield Road, Portree, IV51 9EL. Tel: 01478 612137. Open all year.
Broadford, The Car Park, Broadford, IV49 9AB. Tel: 01471 822361. Seasonal opening.
Dunvegan, 2 Lochside, Dunvegan, IV55 8WB. Tel: 01470 521581. Limited hours during winter.
Uig, Caledonian MacBrayne Ferry Terminal Building, Uig, IV51 9XX. Tel: 01470 542404. Seasonal opening.
Highlands On Line: www.host.co.uk; email: info@host.co.uk

WEATHER FORECASTS

Knowing the weather forecast is useful in planning a day out. Although forecasts can be wrong – and we tend to remember the days when they are – they are far more accurate than in the past. The general forecasts carried on television and radio and in daily newspapers aren't really specific enough for the walker. Much more useful are the outdoor forecasts for walkers and climbers on Radio Scotland at 6.55p.m. on weekdays and 6.25p.m. on Saturdays.

Regular mountain weather forecasts are available by phone. These reports can be obtained as faxes or in spoken form from the following numbers. Be warned though, the charges are high.

Mountaincall West: 0891 500 441
Climbline West Highlands: 0891 654 669

Forecasts can also be found on the World Wide Web. There are several sites. A useful one is www.onlineweather.com/outdoor/mountain

TRANSPORT

Transport map and Highland travel guides are available from:
Roads and Transport, Highland Council, Glenurquhart Road, Inverness, IV3 5NX. Tel: 01463 702695; fax: 01463 702606; email: Sheila.Fletcher@Highland.gov.uk

For local bus times contact:
Skye-Ways Coach Service: Tel:01599 534328; fax: 01599 534862; email: info@skyeways.co.uk; website: www.skyeways.co.uk
Highland Country: Tel: 01463 222244
Scottish CityLink: Tel:08705 505050; website: www.citylink.co.uk
Post Buses Tel: 01463 256273.
Train times Tel: 0345 484950.

USEFUL CONTACTS

John Muir Trust, 41 Commercial Street, Leith, Edinburgh, EH6 6JE. Tel: 0131 554 0114. Website: www.jmt.org.
Mountain Bothies Association, General Secretary, 28 Duke Street, Clackmannan, FK10 4EF. Website: www.mountainbothies.org.uk.
Mountaineering Council of Scotland, The Old Granary, West Mill Street, Perth PH1 5QP. Tel: 01738 638227. Website: www.mountaineering-scotland.org.uk.
Ramblers' Association Scotland, Crusader House, Balgonie Road, Haig Business Park, Markinch, Fife, KY7 7AQ. Tel: 01592 611177.
Ramblers' Association Head Office, 87-90 Albert Embankment, London, SE1 7TW. Tel: 020 7339 8500. Website: www.ramblers.org.uk
Royal Society for the Protection of Birds, Scottish Headquarters, 17 Regent Terrace, Edinburgh, EH7 5BH.
Royal Society for the Protection of Birds, Head Office, The Lodge, Sandy, Bedfordshire, SG19 2DL. Website: www.rspb.org.uk
Scottish Natural Heritage, 12 Hope Terrace, Edinburgh, EH9 2AS.Tel: 0131 554 9797. Website: www.snh.org.uk. Email: enquiries@snh.org.uk
Scottish Rights of Way Society, 10/2 Sunnyside, Edinburgh, EH7 5RA. Tel: 0131 652 2937.
Scottish Wild Land Group, Treasurer/Membership Secretary, 8 Cleveden Road, Kelvinside, Glasgow, G12 0NT.